What Others Are Saying

Every writer who knows Jesus Christ needs to learn from him and discern his answers. With an incredibly helpful transparency and an obvious passion for her Lord, Marlene Bagnull guides the writer to the feet of Jesus to feast on his riches and be filled to overflowing. This book is one of God's gifts to his writers.

> Ethel Herr
> Author/speaker

Marlene Bagnull understands that walking in obedience isn't easy. When you question your call, want to quit, and feel like God could never use you, pick up this book. You'll find a soulmate in these pages, a friend, someone who has walked and is walking this path of being a writer for Him. You will gain wisdom, be encouraged, and find the strength to keep going.

> Susan M. Cameron
> Author

Just when deadline pressures, rejection slips, or broken contracts make me want to sell life insurance instead of manuscripts, I get an encouraging letter or phone call from Marlene. Her talents not only include writing and marketing but the gifts of encouragement and spiritual insight.

> James N. Watkins
> Author, director of Sandy Cove Christian Writers Conference

Write His Answer, first edition, was a wonderful asset to the Christian seeking to better understand his work and place in God's kingdom as a missionary of the written word. This new edition carries forward Marlene's first work of love with added insights and challenges.

> Debbie L. Barker
> Former director of Colorado Christian Writers Conference

Even those of us who have been publishing for years go through times when we need encouragement and a refocusing of our perspective. Marlene provides both in *Write His Answer*. I appreciate the fact that she takes us into God's Word to spend time with Him as well as sharing her own struggles to let us know we're not alone.

Lin Johnson
Managing Editor, *Advanced Christian Writer* and *Church Libraries*
Director, Write-to-Publish Conference
Author/teacher

In focusing on the life and words of Jesus in her excellent book *Write His Answer,* Marlene Bagnull provides a lamp for the path of every writer, regardless of experience.

Jim Russell
President, The Amy Foundation

When Marlene Bagnull shares her heart with writers, we all feel the pulse beat of her love for her Lord and for those of us who, like her, write his answer. How wonderful and remarkable to know she understands and encourages us with such warmth and grace.

Gayle Roper
Author

Real. Compassionate. Honest. These are the words that come to mind after reviewing the new edition of *Write His Answer*. The book beats in rhythm with the writer's heart.

Sandy Brooks
Director, Christian Writers Fellowship International

I keep an excerpt from *Write His Answer* taped to the cabinet next to my desk. When discouragement sets in, when the loneliness of writing and the enormity of the task threaten to overwhelm me, *Write His Answer* spurs me on. I can think of no better resource for helping a writer maintain a biblical perspective than this book.

Linda J. White
Author

This excellent introduction to successful Christian writing gives the beginner an intimate glimpse into the life of a genuine "pro."

Sherwood E. Wirt
Editor Emeritus, *Decision*

Write His Answer

A Bible Study for Christian Writers

Marlene Bagnull

Write Now Publications
Phoenix, Arizona 85013

Unless otherwise noted, all Scripture quotes are taken from *The Living Bible*, © 1971 owned by assignment by Illinois Regional Bank N.A. (as trustee). Used by permission of Tyndale House Publishers, Inc., Wheaton, IL 60189. All rights reserved.

Scripture quotations marked (NIV) are from The Holy Bible, New International Version, copyright © 1973, 1978, 1984 International Bible Society. Used by permission of Zondervan Bible Publishers.

Scripture taken from *THE MESSAGE*, copyright © by Eugene H. Peterson, 1993, 1994, 1995. Used by permission of NavPress Publishing Group.

Scripture quotations marked (AMP) are from The Amplified Bible, Old Testament, copyright 1965, 1987 by The Zondervan Corporation. The Amplified New Testament, copyright 1958, 1987 by The Lockman Foundation.

Scripture quotations marked (TEV) are from Today's English Version (*Good News for Modern Man*) © American Bible Society, 1976. Used by permission.

Scripture quotations marked KJV are from the King James Version.

"Words," page 58, © Sue Cameron, 1993. Used by permission.

"Servants of the Word," page 70, © Mary Nixon, 1997. Used by permission.

Published by Write Now Publications
A royalty division of ACW Press
5501 N. 7th. Ave., #502
Phoenix, Arizona 85013
1-800-931-2665
www.acwpress.com

Publisher's Cataloging-in-Publication
(Provided by Quality Books, Inc.)

Bagnull, Marlene
    Write his answer: a Bible study for Christian writers /
    Marlene Bagnull — 2nd ed.
      p. cm.
    Includes bibliographical references.
    ISBN 1-89252-512-7

    1. Christian literature — Authorship. I. Title.

BR44.B34 1999   248.8'8
                    QBI99-102

Printed in the United States of America
by Bethany Press International
Bloomington, Minnesota

To

My husband, Paul,
who has never once asked,
"Why don't you get a real job?"
His love and support
make it possible
for me to be in full-time ministry.

Anne Sirna, Lee Roddy,
and so many others
who have taught me the
craft of writing
and who have encouraged me
to persevere.

My special friends,
Sue Cameron and Debbie Barker,
who have helped me stretch and grow
and who read this manuscript
and provided valuable insights.

The thousands of writers
I've had the joy and privilege
of encouraging
to write his answer.

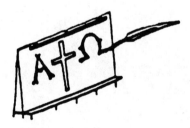

And the Lord said to me,
"Write my answer on a billboard,
large and clear,
so that anyone can read it at a glance
and rush to tell the others."

Habakkuk 2:2

Contents

Foreword

This book can change your life. It not only gives ongoing encouragement to respond to God's call to write but helps you keep on writing. This book can also be used to deepen your walk with him.

I am pleased to introduce you to the book's author, Marlene Bagnull.

I met Marlene at a 1980 writers' conference where I was speaking and teaching. Marlene, like many, felt God's call on her life to write for him.

At that time, I wrote a notation in Marlene's Bible about one of my own motivational passages, Habakkuk 2:2 and 3. There God says to "write the vision." In the margin of Marlene's Bible, alongside those verses, I wrote, "This was God's promise to me as an author. Maybe yours, too?"

Marlene was sure God had called her to write a book, so she set down her vision. That's not uncommon. Many writers, filled with inspiration, start off strong. Then they get discouraged and quit. When they do, God's vision for them is lost. How sad!

If it's God's will to write, then it's logical that publication should eventually follow. After all, an unfinished manuscript cannot change lives. Even a finished one cannot minister in a drawer or filing cabinet. Only in published form can a book go where you and I will never go, to people we will never meet. Only in published form can a book make a difference in eternity.

So why do many writers, feeling called to write, fall short? I believe it's because they neglect to note the way God says he will bring the vision to pass. That involves his time element, not the writer's. Read the Lord's clear words: "But these things I [God] plan won't happen right away. Slowly, steadily, surely, the time approaches when the vision will be fulfilled. If it seems slow, do not despair, for these things will surely come to pass. Just be patient! They will not be overdue a single day!" (Hab. 2:3).

I don't know of a single successful author in the inspirational field who hasn't experienced doubts and discouragement. The unsuccessful are the ones who quit.

Marlene did not quit. She was faithful. She kept her commitment and obeyed her call, even though she suffered through some very, very discouraging times. Hard times. Testing times. Learning times.

God gave Marlene the reward of a published book, then another, plus the seed for this one, and then two others. But this isn't a book about Marlene; it's a book about you, the called writer.

This devotional book for writers (published or unpublished) is designed to inspire and give encouragement for those difficult times that all writers face. It's a work planned to help you fulfill your call and see the fruits of your labors.

Please join Marlene as she leads you through her unique devotionals for writers; for this book can change your life.

LEE RODDY
Penn Valley, CA

Preface to the New Edition

A Few Words to Old Friends and to New

For as long as I can remember, books have been an important part of my life. The twelve volumes of My Book House were among my most treasured possessions when I was a little girl. Through them I entered my own magic kingdom of knights and fair maidens. The creatures of the woodlands became my friends. Places I had never been and people I had never met became real to me because of the power of words.

As a teenager, I opened the most important Book of all. Although King James English wasn't easy for me to understand, my love of words and curiosity to know more about the Author kept me reading. I searched the shelves of my public library for novels that would help me better understand biblical times. I devoured books like *The Silver Chalice*, *Ben-Hur*, and *The Robe*, yearning to know Christ as the characters in them did. Then one day I found a paperback by Jim Bishop, *The Day Christ Died*, in a local store. I wept as I read it. Jesus loved *me* that much! Falling on my knees, I committed my life to him.

That was almost forty years ago and long before I ever suspected that God would channel my love of words into a writing and speaking ministry. Good thing he didn't tell me. I wouldn't have believed him! Who, me?

But why not me? Why not you? "We are God's workmanship, created in Christ Jesus to do good works, which God prepared in advance for us to do" (Eph. 2:10, NIV).

Do you believe it? I do! He knows the plans he has for us and our writing (Jer. 29:11). They're great plans, exciting plans, plans that can make an eternal difference in the lives of our readers.

"Go and make disciples of all nations . . . teaching them to obey everything I have commanded you," the Risen Christ told his followers (Matt. 28:19-20, NIV). Dr. James Russell, president of The Amy Foundation* says, "Our heavenly Father has given us a magnificent proclamation victory. We have responded with a monumental discipling failure." He bases this conclusion on the fact that the Gallup studies indicate 74% of Americans have made a commitment to Jesus Christ and yet our nation "continues an accelerating decline into moral degeneracy."

I believe God is calling us to write his answer. It's time to boldly step out in faith and to write the words that need to be written—powerful words, winsome words, anointed words that will come only by allowing him to speak to our own hearts. And so it is my earnest prayer that as you read this book, you'll make time to do the "Responding to God's Call to Write" section at the end of each chapter. Allow him to speak to you through his Word first. Open your heart to him. Only then will our lives and words "shine out . . . like beacon lights" as we hold out "the Word of Life" (Phil. 2:15-16).

---

*For more information about The Amy Foundation, including various writing awards, The Amy Internet Syndicate, and Church Writing Groups, write to P.O. Box 16091, Lansing, MI 48901; or check out their Web site at www.amyfound.org.

1

Called to Write

"Write my answer on a billboard,
large and clear, so that anyone can read it
at a glance and rush to tell the others."
HABAKKUK 2:2

Our neighborhood was no longer quiet or safe. A group of rowdy teens had claimed it. After a night of their partying, empty beer cans littered our manicured lawns. It was not at all uncommon to find paint sprayed on cars, flat tires, and smashed lawn furniture. The targets of their vandalism were those who dared to suggest they quiet down or go someplace else.

"What next?" we wondered and worried, especially when it became evident that drugs were involved. We knew we should do something, but what? The police regularly patrolled, but they seemed as helpless as we felt.

One night the kid brother of a gang member climbed a pole by the trolley stop and was electrocuted by the wires above the tracks. He was only thirteen! "Oh God," I cried, "was there something I could have done that might have saved his life?"

I've asked similar questions when I've viewed documentaries on homelessness, alcohol and drug addiction, AIDS, child abuse, the aging. The problems are so immense, so beyond my control. And I feel so helpless.

The family—the most basic and important unit of society—is under attack. Christian homes are far from immune. Divorce, adultery, the battering of women and children, incest, and teen suicide devastate *our* homes too. Immorality is rampant. Violent crime, especially in our schools and crimes committed by girls, is increasing. And our children, both before and after birth, are at risk.

Where is God? What is he doing about it? I believe he is calling people like you and like me to "write my answer on a billboard, large and clear, so that anyone can read it at a glance and rush to tell the others" (Hab. 2:2).

When the Lord first brought this verse to my attention in 1979, I was not at all certain he was speaking to me. I knew Jesus Christ as my Lord and Savior. I knew he is the answer to man's deepest needs, but I doubted my ability to write that answer in a compelling and effective way. I had never gone to college or taken a course in creative writing. And I had never shaken the enormous inferiority complex I'd been carrying since childhood. It didn't take me long to conclude that he must have meant that verse for someone else.

Then I recalled a familiar Scripture: "If anyone publicly acknowledges me as his friend, I will openly acknowledge him as my friend before my Father in heaven. But if anyone publicly denies me, I will openly deny him before my Father in heaven" (Matt. 10:32-33).

Certainly my refusal to write was not a denial of him, or was it? "Lord," I prayed, "you know I don't ever want to deny you, but I don't see how I . . ."

"It's not a question of your ability," I felt him assure me. "You can do everything I ask you to do with the help of Christ who will give you the strength and power" (Phil. 4:13).

I tried a whole bunch of "but Lord" excuses. They all sounded hollow next to his promise to help me. "But," I persisted, "I don't even know what you want me to write. I know you are the answer, but how do I say that in a way that someone will publish it?"

"Write out of your life experiences," he said to me. "Make yourself transparent and vulnerable so others can see what I have done, and am doing, in your life."

The choice was clear. The Lord had given me my instructions. To refuse would be an act of disobedience. Yet it wasn't easy to admit on paper, for the world to read, that I often failed to handle problems in a Christlike way. I didn't want people to know that I'm not a model Christian, that my faith falters, and that some days I feel overwhelmed and inadequate. But I also knew the Lord had taught me many things through my struggles—lessons that could perhaps help someone else.

I swallowed my pride and began to write about "Battling and Defeating Depression," "Coping with Ingratitude," and "Praying About Everything." I discovered the answers he'd given me could be a source of help and reassurance to others who also asked, "What's the Matter with Me?" or "How Much Longer, Lord?"

Making myself more vulnerable, I began to write about my life as a wife and mother. I admitted that "It Takes Two to Tangle" and that sometimes I'm guilty of "Taking It Out On the Ones I Love." I sensed the most difficult things for me to share could be the very words someone else needed to read. Yet the more prolific I became, the more my mailbox was stuffed with returned manuscripts. Sometimes they came back faster than I thought the U.S. Postal Service could deliver them! Others, like my first book manuscript, sat on an editor's desk for five months only to be returned with a form rejection slip.

"Do you think it was easy for me to go to the cross?" the Lord asked me one day when I grumbled about the mail. Stung by the truth of his words, I immediately apologized for forgetting how much he had suffered for my salvation.

"Neither is it easy for you to follow in my footsteps," he said gently. "But what I ask you to do, and what I will enable you to do, is to 'put aside your own pleasures and shoulder your cross, and follow me closely. If you insist on saving your life, you will lose it. Only those who throw away their lives for my sake and for the sake of the Good News will ever know what it means to really live'" (Mark 8:34-35).

Real living. From the world's viewpoint, the life of a Christian writer hardly measures up. Few of us will achieve fame or fortune or even earn minimum wage for the hours we sit before our computers. But God sends me reminders when I need them most, often in the form of a thank you from someone who has read something I've written. In light of eternity, low pay and rejection slips mean nothing if even one life is touched.

I still struggle with feelings of inadequacy and self-doubts, but I do *not* doubt the One who has called me. I am choosing to keep my eyes on him and to write his answer. "This is my life work: helping people understand and respond to this Message. It came as a sheer gift to me, a real surprise, God handling all the details. . . . God saw to it that I was equipped, but you can be sure that it had nothing to do with my natural abilities. And so here I am, preaching and writing about things that are way over my head, the inexhaustible riches and generosity of Christ" (Eph. 3:7-8, *The Message*).

～∾

RESPONDING TO GOD'S CALL TO WRITE

God has provided guidelines for writers in Habakkuk 2:2 and related Scriptures. (See Appendix 1, p. 147.) Before moving on to the next chapter, take time to read and meditate on these verses, to allow the Lord to speak to you, and to answer the following questions.

Do I believe God has called me to write his answer? Why or why not?

What issue most deeply concerns me? Is there something God may want to say through me?

What verse in Appendix 1 spoke most powerfully to me? Write it below, and then commit it to memory.

2

Look to Jesus

Keep your eyes on Jesus, our leader and instructor.
HEBREWS 12:2

We are literature missionaries! While we may never go more than a few hundred miles from our homes, our written words can go around the world and make a difference for all eternity.

The opportunities are great. The importance of looking to Jesus, "our leader and instructor" (Heb. 12:2), is even greater. It is his life and death and resurrection that inspires us to keep on keeping on. He provides the pattern we need to follow if we are to be effective communicators of his truth.

Spend time in prayer. While the Gospels give us only glimpses into Jesus' prayer life, it is obvious his ministry was bathed in prayer. Prior to his first preaching tour, he got up long before daybreak in order to go alone into the wilderness and pray (Mark 1:35). In the midst of a demanding ministry, he "often withdrew to the wilderness for prayer" (Luke 5:16). He even spent an entire night in prayer before choosing his twelve disciples (Luke 6:12).

Jesus' example shows us that the place to begin all our writing is on our knees. It is essential that we seek the "mind of Christ" (1 Cor. 2:16) if we hope to bring his answer to our hurting world. If we're too busy to pray, we're too busy. If we think we can shirk this necessary first step, we'll find that our words and paragraphs, no matter how well composed, will lack power. Prayer was an essential part of Jesus' preparation for ministry. So, too, it must be for us.

Know what God's Word says and means. The Bible is silent about Jesus' childhood except for the story of his trip to Jerusalem and how he amazed the teachers of the Law with his understanding of the Scriptures (Luke 2:41-47). After his baptism, Jesus used the Scriptures to defeat Satan (Luke 4:1-12). Throughout his ministry, Jesus often referred to the Law and the Prophets. Unlike the religious people of that day, Jesus "spoke as one who knew the truth, instead of merely quoting the opinions of others as his authority" (Luke 4:32).

Unless we daily spend time in God's Word, our understanding of it will be shallow. Our manuscripts will be filled only with our opinions instead of God's truth. It is the Word of God that convicts and changes people as well as prepares them to face the problems and challenges of daily living (Heb. 4:12; 2 Tim. 3:16-17). Unless we are hungry for God's Word and partake of it daily, we cannot hope to inspire our readers to take it seriously.

Have a vision. Jesus knew why he had come and what he was called to do. Every word he spoke and everything he did was aimed at bringing glory to the Father (John 17:4). He chose to become "obedient to death—even death on a cross!" (Phil. 2:8, NIV).

"Where there is no vision, the people perish" (Prov. 29:18, KJV)—and so do we as writers. We need to wait before the Lord for him to give us direction for our lives and writing ministries. "It's in Christ that we find out who we are and what we are living for" (Eph. 1:12, *The Message*).

Don't cut yourself off from people and their needs. Jesus willingly "laid aside his mighty power and glory, taking the disguise of a slave and becoming like men" (Phil. 2:7). Once here, he did not cloister himself in the Holy of Holies. Instead, he walked and talked, laughed, ate, and wept with those around him. He knew their needs because he was one with them.

There is always a danger that the very nature of our work as writers will cause us to become hermits. It takes time to write, but sometimes we spend too much time writing. Our lives may get out of balance. (See chapter 5.) We need to remember that our words will become glib and empty if we lose touch with people and their needs.

Know your audience and find ways to communicate effectively. Jesus used down-to-earth illustrations from everyday life—a man sowing in his field, a woman baking bread, a widow giving two small coins. He used these examples to bring home his points. Parables, or stories, became Jesus' vehicle for teaching truth on many levels. Even the youngest child could understand the story of the prodigal son or the good Samaritan, yet the depth of these stories and their application to our lives continue to be discovered.

We, too, must know our audience. Are our potential readers young or old? Male or female? Single or married? High school or college graduates? Will the illustrations we use have meaning for them? Are we training ourselves to observe what is happening around us and using these observations to make our points effectively? Are we learning to show instead of tell—in other words, to effectively use stories to present our message?

Jesus used everyday language. His listeners didn't have to be scholars to understand what he was saying. Are we addressing our readers at their level of understanding, being careful not to write down to them but neither to write above their heads? Is our language clear and easy to understand? Most important of all, are we trusting in the mighty power that is present "in the simple message of the cross of Christ" (1 Cor. 1:17); or have we been cluttering it up to impress our readers with our theological prowess and exegetical expertise?

Learn to persist. Some of our work, like that of the most gifted authors, will be rejected. Yet again, we need to look to the Lord and his example.

Jesus' very life's work was rejected by the people he came to save (John 1:10-11). Because it was no easier for Jesus than it is for us, he understands and "is wonderfully able to help us" (Heb. 2:18; cf. Heb. 2:17; 4:15). Beyond that, he has given us his promise that in and through him we will do even greater things than he did (John 14:12). As we ask him for help and seek to follow his example, our writing and our lives will be an inspiration to others.

RESPONDING TO GOD'S CALL TO WRITE

What priority do I give to prayer? (See Psalm 5:3; Colossians 4:2; 1 Thessalonians 5:17.)

What priority do I give to God's Word? (See Psalm 1:2; James 1:22-25.)

Have I sought the Lord for a vision for my writing? If so, am I walking in obedience to that vision? (See Psalm 25:4-5.)

How much am I in touch with people and their needs? (See Philippians 2:4.)

How often do I rewrite each manuscript until it is my very best work with no wasted words or weak phrases? (See 2 Timothy 2:15.)

Am I willing to persist, or do I expect the Lord to somehow make it easy? (See Hebrews 10:36.)

3

Making It Happen

*Make a careful exploration of who you are
and the work you have been given,
and then sink yourself into that.*
GALATIANS 6:4, THE MESSAGE

"I am the Bread of Life. I am the Light of the world. I am the Good Shepherd." Jesus did not have an identity crisis! He knew who he was and why he had come. Regardless of circumstances or the opinions of others, he affirmed that he was the great "I Am" who existed before Abraham.

There are many "I ams" we can also affirm. We have no problem with some: I am a son or daughter, a father or mother. Neither do we have difficulty with such "I ams" as I am a member of Fifth Street Church or the PTA.

As Christians, we can affirm still others: I am a believer. I am saved. I am forgiven. But as we move into the area of feelings and life goals, our "I ams" tend to become cloudy. I am a witness for Christ might be prefaced by "sometimes." And even if we know God has called us to write, the statement, "I am a writer," might stick in our throats or be qualified by such words as "I think" or "I hope to be." Even established writers have days when they don't feel like writers—days when the fruit of their labors may not seem evident.

Each spring I'm out in my garden as soon as the soil is no longer frozen. As I drop seeds into holes and push dirt around tender seedlings, I envision the bouquets of zinnias and daisies I will pick for my dining room table. So, too, we also need to envision the writer we hope to become and the work we hope to produce for the Lord's glory. More importantly, we need to envision the writer God wants us to become.

I'm not talking about using visualization techniques but rather a biblical principle: "What he thinks is what he really is" (Prov. 23:7, TEV). I've seen it proven many times. When I would get up on the wrong side of the bed and picture myself becoming irritable with the children and getting nothing accomplished, my expectations were not disappointed. My children are now grown, but the principle is still the same. What I think in my heart is what I become! But what is true of negative thoughts is also true of positive ones. When my mind is centered on Christ and I choose to rely on "his mighty power," I discover he "is able to do far more" than my "highest prayers, desires, thoughts, or hopes" (Eph. 3:20).

Making it happen involves more than just desiring to see it happen. It also takes realistic and planned action. Periodically I take time apart with the Lord to assess where I'm at and where I need to be heading. I find it helpful first to set long-range goals. What is God's overall plan and purpose for my writing? Where does he want me to be five years from now? Then I break down that plan into specific and measurable short-term goals. When I first started writing, those goals included growing in my Christian walk, keeping a journal, studying the craft of writing, researching the markets, and completing my first manuscript. The first four goals have been, and must be, ongoing. I have frequently changed and enlarged that fifth one to reflect new writing challenges.

It has been said, "Attempt something so big that without God's help it will surely fail." In other words, we need to stretch beyond our comfort zones if we're to discover the joy-filled reality of "quietly depending upon the Lord for his help, and not on our own skills" (2 Cor. 1:12).

Next, it's time to take a big step of faith and verbalize our goals to others. That's scary! I remember the first year I went to a Christian writers' conference and told people about the book I planned to get published. Although it must have been obvious that

I had a lot to learn before I could hope to write—much less sell—a book, the instructors encouraged me to work at it. Other writers promised to pray for me.

Another step in reaching our goals is to determine the necessary spiritual and practical preparation. Do we need to become more disciplined in our study of God's Word? Are we actively involved in a strong body of believers? Practical preparation might include taking an English refresher course, attending a local creative writing class, enrolling in a correspondence study program (see page 169), joining or forming a writers' critique group (see page 161), or attending a conference.

Anticipating obstacles and how I will overcome them is another important step. For instance, the telephone is one of mine. I love to talk, and I hate answering machines. I said I would *never* get one. Instead, I tried monitoring the length of my calls during business hours. I tried and failed! I've found that an answering machine is a necessary time-saver. So is the computer I said I never wanted.

I find it is essential to regularly review my goals. Tucked away in a bottom drawer, they will be useless. But more important than whether or not we realize our goals and sell x number of manuscripts is the manner in which we do our work and the foundation on which we build our writing ministry. We can never become so consumed by our goals—by what we want to do for the Lord—that we neglect what he wants to do with us.

Prayerfully setting goals, putting them in writing, sharing them with others, and determining the specific things we need to do to make them happen is just the beginning. Then, as David told Solomon when he gave him the blueprints for the temple, we must "be strong and courageous and get to work. Don't be frightened by the size of the task, for the Lord my God is with you; he will not forsake you. He will see to it that everything is finished correctly" (1 Chron. 28:20).

I am a writer! I am endeavoring to present the Good News of Jesus Christ through the words I write. I am matching my prayers with hard work. When I get discouraged, I remind myself to claim his promises and trust him to make it happen. (See "A Writer's Statement of Faith" on page 159.)

RESPONDING TO GOD'S CALL TO WRITE

Proverbs 16:9 says, "We should make plans—counting on God to direct us." Enlarge the goal planning chart below; then go before the Lord and ask him to show you what he wants you to do (Jer. 29:11-13). And remember, "Pray that he'll fill your good ideas and acts of faith with his own energy so that it all amounts to something" (2 Thess. 1:11, *The Message*).

GOAL PLANNING CHART

	Specific Goals	Spiritual Preparation	Practical Preparation	Expected Obstacles	How I Will Overcome
Weekly					
Monthly					
One Year					
Five Years					

4

How Can I Know God Has Called Me?

If you want to know what God wants you to do,
ask him, and he will gladly tell you.

JAMES 1:5

I remember the year I sobbed through the closing session of the St. Davids Christian Writers' Conference. I had come to the conference with such high expectations. God had provided the money and baby-sitters. Surely, just as he had opened the door for me to come, he would also open the door for the publication of my book manuscript. But none of the editors I talked with that week expressed interest, and the article I had worked so hard on for the contest was not a winner.

"Why don't you just give up?" the Evil One hissed. "You don't have what it takes. You're only setting yourself up for heartache. What makes you think God can use you anyway?"

Several years and about thirty rejection slips later, the book I had tried so hard to sell at that conference was finally accepted for publication. What enabled me to persevere? I knew that I knew God had called me to write. I clung to the promise that I would be "rooted deeply in the soil and bear fruit for God" (2 Kings 19:30). And God faithfully honored his promise. The winds of doubt and testing, rather than uprooting me, have caused my roots to "grow down into him and draw up nourishment from him" (Col. 2:7).

In the fifteen years I've been teaching at Christian writers' conferences, over and over again wannabe writers have asked me, "How can I know God has called me to write?" It's a crucial question! Those who are the most gifted, those whom I sense are truly called, are the ones who struggle the most to find God's answer. They are the ones Satan especially targets because they are a genuine threat to his agenda.

How can we be certain God has called us to write?

Desire to know his will. While this statement seems like an obvious first step, the truth is we may be afraid to ask him. I remember how difficult it was to surrender my hopes and dreams and lay my book on the altar, repeatedly, during the six years of trying to find a publisher. It wasn't easy to pray "not my will, but thine."

Although painful, the death of a vision is a necessary prerequisite to resurrection. We can know God's will only when we stop asking him to bless what we've already made up our minds to do and simply pray, "Tell me where you want me to go and I will go there" (Ps. 86:11). Only then will the truth of Psalm 37:4 (NIV) become reality in our lives: "Delight yourself in the Lord and he will give you the desires of your heart."

Be open to God's surprises, to the new thing he may want to do in and through you. If anyone had told me when I was in high school that one day I would be in a full-time writing and speaking ministry, I would have said, "A loving God would *never* do that to me!" I died a thousand deaths every time I had to give a speech in the required public speaking class, and I hated English with a passion.

God says, "This plan of mine is not what you would work out, neither are my thoughts the same as yours!" (Isa. 55:8). How true! His plan is far more exciting.

How can we know God's calling? One way, but *not* the only way, is when surprising doors open—doors that we could not open and cannot walk through in our own strength.

Deepen our relationship with him. Paul and I have been married almost thirty-five years. We've come to know each other so well that we frequently anticipate what the other is about to say. God longs for us to develop the same closeness with him. "Take care to live in me, and let me live in you," Jesus said. "For a branch can't produce fruit when severed from the vine. Nor can you be fruitful apart from me" (John 15:4). But what kind of fruit?

Ask him. Again, this step seems so obvious; and yet, sadly, many believers have not learned to hear his voice. As Peter Lord points out in *Hearing God* (Grand Rapids: Baker, 1988), Jesus' most repeated phrase is, "He who has ears to hear, let him hear."

God is not playing cat and mouse or the "now you're getting warmer, now you're cold" game we may have played as children. He desires for us to know and do his will, but he will not send a fax or an e-mail message. He expects us to ask and to listen, "for he is always ready to give a bountiful supply of wisdom to all who ask him; he will not resent it. But when you ask him, be sure that you really expect him to tell you, for a doubtful mind will be as unsettled as a wave of the sea that is driven and tossed by the wind; and every decision you then make will be uncertain, as you turn first this way, and then that. If you don't ask with faith, don't expect the Lord to give you any solid answer" (James 1:5-8).

Look for and expect God's guidance and confirmation of your call. "The Scriptures outline four channels for guidance: the Word of God, the inward promptings of the Spirit, the ordering of circumstances, and counsel of godly Christians," Mark Porter says in *The Time of Your Life* (Wheaton, IL: Victor, 1983, p. 27).

We need to search the Scriptures daily, prefacing our study by asking God to speak to us. I find it helpful to write down the passages that jump out at me. In times of doubt and discouragement, they are the assurance that God has indeed called me and will equip me to write.

Someone has said Satan cannot counterfeit God's peace. In view of this fact, an important part of determining God's will is the presence or absence of this peace. When words are not flowing and nothing is selling, do we still have a quietness within that writing is what God wants us to do? When we are tempted to quit, do we feel the inward prompting of the Spirit to continue? Do we have a lack of peace until we again pick up our pens?

It's unlikely that God will so order the circumstances of our lives that we have nothing else to do but write! But he may confirm he has called us to write through what my friend, Chaplain Charlie, calls "God incidents." Someone may give us stamps when we have no money for postage. A word of encouragement or acceptance may come just at the time we are ready to call it quits. Be careful, however, not to overly rely on God incidents and put the Lord to a test (Matt. 4:7).

As for godly counsel, Proverbs 15:22 (TEV) says, "Get all the advice you can, and you will succeed; without it you will fail." To pursue a ministry of writing without the support and prayers of mature Christians is as foolhardy as a soldier advancing against the enemy with no one covering him.

For some writers, knowing they are called is a one-time turning point the same as their conversions. For others, it is a steadily growing knowing that this is what God wants them to do. Regardless, as my friend Sue Cameron says, "We can know with certainty that we are in the center of his will when he receives the glory, others receive grace, and we receive joy!"

≈≥©

Responding to God's Call to Write

Read James 1:5-8. Are you ready to receive a "solid answer" from the Lord regarding your call to write? If so, record here what he tells you.

5

Keeping in Balance

~≈©~

God, help me to understand what you want me to do today;
make me wise about spiritual things;
and help me to live this day
in a way that will please and honor you.
COLOSSIANS 1:9–10, AUTHOR'S PARAPHRASE

My father- and mother-in-law are two of my favorite people. Because they live almost 400 miles away, we never see enough of them, yet I remember one time they visited when I simply could not relax and enjoy them. Instead, I almost wished they would leave so that I could get to work on an idea for an article. Sadly, I had allowed my work as a writer to become too important and consuming. Once again, it had gotten out of balance with my other priorities.

I knew God had called me to write. I also knew that unless I found a more balanced way to pursue my writing, my whole family would suffer. Although I had the self-discipline to work twelve-hour days, I was not any more fruitful than the writer who lacks discipline and works only sporadically. I was not producing quality material, nor was I giving my family—or anyone or anything else—quality time. My long hours created little more than physical, mental, emotional, and spiritual fatigue. Obviously, I had a lot to learn about being driven or led (see chapter 31) as well as about prioritizing and keeping in balance.

The Bible says, "Fear God—know that He is, revere and worship Him—and keep His commandments" (Eccl. 12:13, AMP). In the midst of trying to serve God, I again forgot the importance of my relationship with him and others. I had given too high a priority to my work and put an unbalanced emphasis on Romans 12:11: "Never be lazy in [my] work but serve the Lord enthusiastically."

Because writing is work, work that must be done in God's way if we want God's blessing, it is important to periodically assess the way we approach our work as writers. Is the effectiveness of our writing ministry being hindered because we are inclined to overwork? Does our writing consume too much of our time and energy? Are we *Keeping the Sabbath Wholly* as Marva Dawn asks in her must-read book (Grand Rapids: Eerdmans, 1995)? With multiple demands on our time, how can we order our priorities and keep our lives in balance?

My writing mentor, Anne Sirna, gave me some valuable insights. "Life is like a table with four legs," she said. "If any one of those legs is too long or too short, the table is wobbly."

"And my work as a writer is just one of those legs," I observed, "yet I've allowed it to unbalance my whole life." Out of our conversation came the decision to make the time to pray in depth—not just about my writing, but about my entire life.

First of all, I acknowledged that my table, my life, had to rest on God and his Word. My faith couldn't be one of the legs—it had to be the foundation. My relationship with God had to permeate every area of my life. As *The Message* says, "Anyone who tries to live by his own effort, independent of God, is doomed to failure" (Gal. 3:10).

What about the legs of my table? The Lord showed me three others, besides my writing, that I too often overlooked in my zeal to write his answer.

My family, of course, is one of the legs. All the help my writing might provide others would be worth nothing if I failed my own family. My responsibility as a wife and mother is more than just doing things for them; it is doing things with them. I must guard against my tendency to become preoccupied with my work and must make a conscious decision to be there for them—to give them my full attention and to really listen to what they are saying *and* not saying. Children grow so quickly. Don't sacrifice them on your writing altar.

Extended family, friends, and even strangers are another leg. God reminded me that my life would never be in balance if I became a hermit. I could not allow my response to the Great Commission to be only that of writing words to a faceless audience. I also had something to give people face-to-face, and they had something to give me. The joy of developing close friendships, of discipling and being discipled, must not be given up for long hours alone in front of the computer.

Finally, I saw that the last, but not the least, leg is myself. "Perhaps it's time to learn, again, that the entire world doesn't rest on your shoulders, and that recreation—think of it as re-creation— is also part of God's plan," another wise friend counseled me.

I knew she was right. I need time for myself—for things I enjoy doing, other than work. Not only can taking breaks increase my productivity, I cannot expect to be whole, or to write anything to help others become whole, if I never have any time just for me. I cannot allow my life to get so out of balance that I never have time to play.

I still follow the proverb that says, "Commit your work to the Lord, then it will succeed" (Prov. 16:3); but I'm learning that does not mean I need to be a superwoman. I'm finding *The Living Bible's* paraphrase of Philippians 4:13 helpful: "I can do everything *God asks me to* with the help of Christ who gives me the strength and power" (italics added). As I listen, really listen, for his instructions, he helps me keep in balance.

～⊚

RESPONDING TO GOD'S CALL TO WRITE

Make time for the Lord to speak to you through Proverbs 2:3-10. Then answer the following questions.

Is my writing in the proper balance with the rest of my priorities?

Which legs make up the table of my life?

What one specific thing can I do today to get, or to stay, in balance?

PRESSURES, PRIORITIES, AND PRAISE

Pressures . . .
> to produce,
> to perform,
> to be more and do more
> than is realistic or possible.

Priorities . . .
> demanding my attention,
> pulling me in multiple directions,
> creating guilt
> as I fail to properly order them.

Yet praise . . .
> my God knows and understands.
> He promises peace in the midst,
> and teaches me how to rest in him.

6

Decision Making

❧

For with you is the fountain of life;
in your light we see light.
PSALM 36:9, NIV

You *know* God has called you to write, but you still have many questions and decisions to make. You are discovering it is not enough to know *where* you are going; you need to know *how* to get there.

What road does God want you to travel? Should you write for the religious or secular press? Should you write fiction or nonfiction? Should you write for children or adults? Is God calling you to write a book or short stories or articles? What should you, can you, give up to make time to write?

What about the preparations for your journey we talked about in chapter 3? Do you need to go back to school? Is a degree necessary? Or what about a correspondence course? If so, which one? What about a writers' conference? They cost so much money. Should you, in faith, claim that God will provide? Or are conferences and schooling unrealistic in light of your present financial needs and obligations?

You are bombarded with decisions. But how can you *know* that you've made the right one? How can you be certain of the specifics of God's will?

I remember a particularly intense struggle over a decision I needed to make that would have greatly altered my writing ministry. "Lord," I prayed, "either open or close the door in accord with your will." That seemed like a wise and godly prayer. I wouldn't have to wonder whether or not I had made the right decision. God would make the decision for me. But when the door opened, I didn't have peace about walking through it.

I searched his Word for guidance but found none. I didn't hear His Spirit speaking to my heart. Friends gave me conflicting advice. And as for circumstances—I didn't know whether the open door was a true "God incident" or simply a coincident.

I was in a state of turmoil as the time came close for my final decision. I also felt angry and hurt that God appeared to be leaving me to muddle through it by myself. I wanted to do his will. Why didn't he clearly tell me what he wanted me to do? Why didn't he give me a sign?

In retrospect, I can see that my desire for a quick, easy answer would have robbed me of the following valuable lessons in decision making.

Seek wisdom. There is a condition to his promise. "Yes, if you want better insight and discernment, and are searching for them as you would for lost money or hidden treasure, then wisdom will be given you" (Prov. 2:3-4). I have to admit, I was lazy!

My search began by using the brain God gave me. I looked at the facts and made a list of the pros and cons. But they were almost equal! Obviously my own understanding was insufficient. I needed to acknowledge my need for the Lord and trust him to "make [my] paths straight" (Prov. 3:6, NIV).

"Search me, O God, and know my heart; test me and know my anxious thoughts" (Ps. 139:23, NIV), I prayed as I looked at my list and tried to discover if I had placed the pros and cons in the right columns. Were my motives pure? Was pride or the need to prove myself clouding my perspective?

Then God reminded me that he "grants wisdom! His every word is a treasure of knowledge and understanding" (Prov. 2:6). I studied the list closer and saw changes I needed to make in light of some biblical principles I had been overlooking. I put a star beside those pros and cons that clearly lined up with God's Word. Yet still it was not evident what choice I should make. If anything, I was even more confused.

Surrender. God used my turmoil to speak to me about the importance of surrendering my will to him. I thought I had, but suddenly I saw I hadn't given him my conceptions about what this opportunity would or would not do for my writing career. I had said I wanted his will, but all the while I was busy trying to figure out what would be best for me. It hadn't occurred to me that surrendering might mean making the choice that would appear to be the wrong choice. It might require me to lay down all my goals and dreams. I might not *like* the new direction the Lord would take me. But would I be willing to follow?

I gulped. Those were hard admissions. I could only trust that "God is at work within [me], helping [me] want to obey him, and then helping [me] do what he wants" (Phil. 2:13).

Pray expectantly. In a new way I was now ready for another important lesson—learning to pray expectantly. "Ask, and you will be given what you ask for. Seek, and you will find. Knock, and the door will be opened," Jesus said (Matt. 7:7). As I did ask him to reveal his will—repeatedly, during a long and almost sleepless night—I began to feel his peace. He gave me no signs or visions, but by the time I finally dosed off, a sense of expectancy was growing within me that he would give me the guidance I needed.

God did not disappoint me. The next morning I awoke knowing what he wanted me to do. I had peace! I was tired but exhilarated. The lessons learned had been worth the days of struggle.

Are you having a hard time making a decision? Are you uncertain about what God wants you to do? Seek wisdom, surrender your will to the Lord, and pray expectantly with your ears and eyes open for his answer. In his perfect timing, God will turn your darkness into light. And in his strength you will be able to scale any wall (Ps. 18:28-29).

RESPONDING TO GOD'S CALL TO WRITE

What is God saying to you from the decisions of these men and women of faith?

Abraham (Gen. 12:1-4):

Moses (Ex. 18:13-27):

Joshua (Josh. 24:14-15):

Ruth (Ruth 1:15-17):

David (Ps. 13):

DECISIONS

I don't know which way to turn.
The pros and cons almost balance.
I pray for guidance,
but receive no answer—
no clear direction.
Friends only add to my confusion.
Suddenly I hear him say,
"Follow me."
I see clearly
what I failed to see before.
I don't have to know where I'm going.
He knows!
As long as I stay close to him,
I'll not lose my way
or fail to reach my destination.

7

Learning to Wait

~⊙~

Be still before the Lord and wait patiently for him.
PSALM 37:7, NIV

I groaned as I picked up my mail. My book manuscript had been returned—again. The news at the typewriter repair shop wasn't any better. My typewriter [yes, I began writing on a typewriter] was obsolete and couldn't be repaired. We couldn't afford to replace it. "At least I've got a week to figure out what to do," I told myself as I packed for a much-needed vacation.

Our vacation flew by with no clear direction from the Lord. I knew he was calling me to write, but he sure wasn't giving me answers for my present dilemma. When I got home, things went from bad to worse. I was greeted with a bundle of mail that contained twenty-one returned manuscripts—including the story I had hoped would win the Guideposts Writers' Workshop.

"Oh Lord," I sighed. "I'm tired of trying and yet failing, of waiting and hoping, only to be disappointed."

Choosing to ignore the advice I readily give others—don't waste time feeling sorry for yourself but get those manuscripts back in the mail and then work on a new idea—I walked out of my office, slamming the door behind me. In other words, I had a temper tantrum! As I was fixing myself a snack in the kitchen (something else I shouldn't have been doing), I felt the Lord's presence and his unmistakable voice speaking to me within.

"The lessons I'm trying to teach you, Child, are more important than the sale of hundreds of manuscripts."

"But Lord," I began to object, as I often do.

"Peace. Be still," he said firmly.

In an unexplainable way, the churning within me ceased. I knew he was going to show me something important.

"I want you to learn to wait patiently, productively, and expectantly," he said.

I pondered those words the rest of the day. The productive and expectant part sounded okay. But patience? Surely the Lord knew I had a problem being patient. So, too, I realized, do a lot of others—even the patriarchs of Scripture.

At age seventy-five, Abram left his people and his homeland. "Go to the land I will guide you to. If you do," God promised, "I will cause you to become the father of a great nation" (Gen. 12:1-2). The Bible doesn't tell us how long it took Abram to reach Canaan; but traveling on foot with his flocks and entire household, it wasn't an overnight journey. The fulfillment of the other part of the promise took twenty-five years of waiting and wondering. After all, his wife was barren and wasn't getting younger. But even though they ran ahead of the Lord and created a legacy of problems that still exist today, God, in his perfect timing, honored his promise and blessed them with a son.

I thought of Jacob, waiting and working fourteen years for Rachel to be his wife, and the years the people of Israel waited for God to free them from slavery in Egypt. And then there were the forty years of wandering when it must have seemed like they would *never* reach the Promised Land.

It's a question of whether or not I trust the Lord and his timing. Do I really believe that he knows the plans he has for me, that "they are plans for good and not for evil, to give [me] a future and a hope" (Jer. 29:11)? If God's people in Babylonian captivity believed this promise, why couldn't I? How much more confirmation did I need that God was calling me to write? But, as always, I wanted him to make things happen quickly and easily. Then I saw, in a new way, how God did not shorten the time of waiting even for the birth of his Son.

How difficult those nine months must have been for Mary. There was the fear of whether or not Joseph would believe her story. If he chose not to, she knew he could accuse her of adultery. The penalty would have been death by stoning.

Even when God intervened and assured Joseph that the child had been conceived by the Holy Spirit, Mary still had to face the wagging tongues of the townspeople. I can imagine the pain she must have experienced daily as she went to the well and was ostracized by women who had once been her friends. And there was the very real and difficult wait of those last weeks—the uncomfortable and long journey to Bethlehem on a donkey, the search for lodging, and the hours of labor.

I wonder what lessons Mary learned during that time. Were they ones that prepared her to face her Son's death on a cross? Certainly the lesson of patience—of trusting the Lord to bring about all he had promised—must have been one. I also suspect that she learned to use those months productively, preparing in practical ways for the birth and care of her Son. And throughout that time of waiting, there was undoubtedly a thread of expectancy—of awe that God was permitting her to be a part of his plan.

There are parallels for myself and my work as a writer. If I fail to learn the lesson of patience, I won't be prepared to persist during other dry spells. The challenge Lee Roddy once gave me, "write so heaven will be different," will never happen if my lack of patience causes me to quit.

If I choose to use waiting times to indulge in self-pity and gripe to other writers about "those editors," time that could be used productively will be lost.

And finally, failing to learn to wait expectantly will be the denial of a Scripture I promised years ago to heed. "I will keep on expecting you to help me. I [will] praise you more and more. I [will] walk in the strength of the Lord God" (Ps. 71:14, 16)—through the times when my writing is bearing fruit, as well as through the times when I must wait for it to mature and ripen.

RESPONDING TO GOD'S CALL TO WRITE

If your writing ministry seems to be on hold, ask the Lord, "What are you trying to teach me?" Be still in his presence. Then write his answer here.

Think of specific things you can do to wait patiently, productively, and expectantly. List them below.

Read the following passages: Psalm 27:14; 32:8; 42:11; 130:3-6; Isaiah 40:29-31; Hebrews 11:1. Which passage most directly speaks to your need today? Begin the process of memorizing it by writing it below and on a card to post above your computer.

8

By My Spirit

"But when the Holy Spirit has come upon you,
you will receive power to testify about me with great effect."
ACTS 1:8

The events of the past week had left the disciples reeling. Their Master had entered Jerusalem thronged by a crowd shouting, "Hosanna!" Less than a week later, another crowd shouted, "Crucify him." He left Jerusalem carrying a cross.

Then the impossible happened. Jesus rose from the dead! They saw him, touched him, broke bread with him. He was alive! And he had commissioned them to "go and make disciples in all the nations" (Matt. 28:19).

The power of the Resurrection and its call to commit ourselves to the living Christ has not diminished in 2,000 years. One Easter, after an intense struggle, I surrendered my life to the Lord and took the plunge into the baptismal waters. Each year since, Easter has been a special time of renewing my commitment to share the Good News that Jesus is alive. He is "the Way—yes, and the Truth and the Life" (John 14:6).

But what happens to my commitment and enthusiasm—and yours, too, perhaps—during the times between our mountaintop experiences? How do we rekindle our resolve to go into the world through our writing when it seems like everything we write is being rejected? Where do we find the determination and strength to per-severe—to keep writing, keep submitting, and keep believing our words will one day get into print?

Jesus knew his disciples well. He knew they were just ordinary men who would need extraordinary power for the task before them. It wasn't going to be easy to reach a world. Although many would believe and be saved, countless others would be threatened and infu-riated by the message of the Cross. In their own strength, the disciples could not hope to endure the persecution that awaited them.

Even after Jesus' resurrection, the disciples had plenty of ques-tions and doubts—the same as us. I suspect some must have felt panicky when Jesus ascended into heaven. Now what? How could they do what he called them to do without him beside them?

"But when the Holy Spirit has come upon you, you will receive power to testify about me with great effect," Jesus promised (Acts 1:8). The message to us is clear. If the men and women who walked and talked with Jesus needed the Holy Spirit, how much more do we need him today!

We need him to sanctify us—to make us holy and acceptable vessels through which Jesus Christ can work (Rom. 15:16; 1 Cor. 6:11). Often uncertain of the direction we should go, we need his guidance (Gal. 5:16). In the face of disappointment and discourage-ment, and some days maybe even despair, we need his comfort (John 14:16) and the gift of hope (Rom. 15:13).

Challenged by conflicting theologies and the subtlety of humanistic ideas, we are dependent on him to reveal God's truth (John 14:17; 15:26; 16:13). We must first be taught if we are to teach others. We are dependent on the Spirit to bring to our attention the lessons we have learned and to show us how to effectively share them with our readers (John 14:26). We need "the Holy Spirit's words to explain the Holy Spirit's facts" (1 Cor. 2:13). We need the "thoughts and mind of Christ" (1 Cor. 2:16) to write with sensitiv-ity and understanding. And, tempted to preach, we need to be reminded that he alone convicts people of their sin and offers them the hope of God's redemption (John 16:8).

Standing in need of all the above and more, the question becomes, "Do we wait long enough to receive everything God wants to give us?" The disciples waited in prayer in the Upper Room for several days after Jesus' ascension. To be honest, I find it difficult to wait even for several minutes.

Far too often, my writing time is prefaced by only a quick token prayer. I ask for the Lord's help and his Spirit's anointing, but I fail to wait for him to fill me. I fail to heed the literal translation of Ephesians 5:18 to "keep on being filled with the Holy Spirit." Even though it's evident that I "leak"—that I need repeated fillings of the Spirit's power—I don't sit still long enough for him to pour himself into me.

If we truly want God's power to infuse our writing and every aspect of our lives, we must learn to wait quietly in his presence. *The Message* says, "Hold your minds in a state of undistracted attention" (2 Pet. 3:1). But I have a hard time being quiet! I'm almost always on the go, always rushing. Even when I do sit still, my mind isn't still. Yet I know I cannot sidestep the importance of first being filled if I hope to write anything that will have a lasting impact. I need his anointing so that every word, every sentence, is written with "the strength and energy that God supplies, so that God will be glorified through Jesus Christ" (1 Pet. 4:11).

The ways each of us experience the power of the Holy Spirit will be unique, just as the gifts he gives us will be different. "There are many ways in which God works in our lives," Paul wrote the Corinthians, "but it is the same God who does the work in and through all of us who are his" (1 Cor. 12:6). We don't need to compare ourselves with anyone else or covet anyone else's gift because "Christ has given each of us special abilities—whatever he wants us to have out of his rich storehouse of gifts" (Eph. 4:7).

God longs for us to come into his presence, to open and to use the gifts he gives us. By his Spirit we, too, can be his witnesses—in our Jerusalem, Judea, Samaria, and even to the ends of the earth (Acts 1:8).

～◎

RESPONDING TO GOD'S CALL TO WRITE

Study the following passages. Beside each reference, note what the Holy Spirit is promising to do in your life. Then ask yourself if you are experiencing this aspect of being filled with the Spirit.

John 14:15-16:

John 14:17, 26; 15:26; 16:13-14:

Romans 15:13:

Romans 15:16; 1 Corinthians 6:11:

1 Corinthians 2:4, 10-16:

Galatians 5:16:

Galatians 5:22-23:

I Don't Understand

Lord, I don't understand
how your Spirit can dwell within me.
I don't understand
how he can change and sanctify me.
But I do understand
why I need
all you have for me.
Thank you for meeting me
at my point of weakness,
for filling me with your power
to be all you call me to be.

9

Overcoming Procrastination

*Dreaming instead of doing is foolishness,
and there is ruin in a flood of empty words.*
ECCLESIASTES 5:7

I sighed as I read the note at the bottom of the printed rejection slip: "I'm sorry, but we recently purchased a similar manuscript."

This wasn't the first time I'd missed out on a sale because I'd waited too long to develop an idea and get it in the mail. Like many writers, I tend to procrastinate. I am a typical Type A personality, an achiever, a true workaholic. Yet when I stop long enough to evaluate my accomplishments, I know that I have not always done, or written, that which is most important in the Lord's eyes.

The Merriam Webster Dictionary defines procrastination: "To put off usually habitually the doing of something that should be done." While some procrastinate more than others, few of us (if we are honest) can say we never procrastinate. For a myriad of reasons, we put off doing things—especially, it seems, getting words on paper. It's no wonder God seems to call a number of people to write similar things. He knows how few will actually finish what they start.

"O Lord, you have examined my heart and know everything about me," I read in Psalm 139:1. I cannot hide my problem of procrastinating from him, but I can go to him for help to overcome it.

The first step to victory comes by facing the reasons why I procrastinate. Sometimes, to be honest, it's laziness. Writing is hard work! It's easier to talk about it than to do it. But since I know writing is the work God has called me to do, I need to do it.

Sometimes I procrastinate because I'm overextended. I have difficulty saying no. All too often my time and energy are drained as I allow my priorities to get out of order. And then there's the "tyranny of the urgent." I'm ruled by my never-ending to-do list that is filled with things that seem to demand my attention but have no eternal significance.

Other times, I procrastinate because of a problem with my will. I know what God has called me to do, but I choose to do what I want. It's not easy for me to discipline myself to stay in my office when it's a beautiful day outside or when a friend calls and wants to chat. Even though I usually win that battle because I enjoy working, I still may not end up accomplishing what God wants me to do.

An editor gave me a go-ahead on a book proposal. I told him I would have the manuscript to him in three months. Then I began procrastinating! I decided I could work more efficiently if I reorganized my files. Then I got sidetracked answering letters and reworking manuscripts that had been sitting around for months. Doing so got me in the mood to market my returned manuscripts. I convinced myself they really should get back in the mail. Before I realized it, a month had passed without even five minutes spent on the book manuscript. Why? The biggest reason I procrastinate is because I'm afraid of failure.

Facing the reasons why I procrastinate doesn't make me feel good, but it is a prerequisite to the second step to victory—confession. My good intentions are not enough. They do not get me off the hook.

Jesus told a parable about a man with two sons (Matt. 21:28-32). He asked both of them to go and work in the vineyard. The first son said he wouldn't, but later he changed his mind and did what his father asked. The second son said he would, but he didn't. Did he deliberately break his word or simply procrastinate?

When God calls something to my attention, it's not what I say I will do that counts—it's what I actually do. "Knowing what is right to do and then not doing it [this includes procrastination!] is sin" (James 4:17). It is only as I confess this sin and realize my worthlessness before the Lord that he lifts me up, encourages, and helps me (James 4:8-10). While some opportunities may be gone forever, God does not leave me in the land of regrets. He redeems the time I've lost and gives me another chance (Prov. 28:13).

The third step to victory requires that I risk being open and honest with other Christians—especially other Christian writers. "Admit your faults to one another and pray for each other," James 5:16 says. That's not an easy thing to do. Yet people cannot pray on target for my needs if they don't know what they are. It has been a tremendous help and encouragement to know that others are praying for me—and holding me accountable to do the things I've committed myself to do.

Other steps I have taken to overcome procrastination include memorizing Scripture promises, reexamining my priorities, and making lists. (I'm an endless list maker; but as my husband points out, that doesn't necessarily mean that what is on my list will ever get done!) I have even used a system of rewards and punishments, "earning" the right to do the things I want to do by first doing the thing I would prefer to put off. Some methods help. Others do not. But I am finding that the most important step after self-examination, confession, and seeking the prayer support of others is such a simple one I often overlook it. At the beginning of each day I need to ask, "Lord, what do you want me to do?"

When I allow the Lord to be Lord of my schedule and my daily to-do list, I am less prone to procrastinate. Minute-by-minute obedience pleases God. It also frees me from the frustration of being torn in different directions by my unrealistic expectations and the resulting burden of guilt. As I leave my schedule to the Lord, he brings order to what would otherwise be chaos and peace to what would otherwise be confusion.

God knows what needs to take priority in my life at any given moment. He shows me those priorities when I stop long enough to ask him (and) to wait for his response. He may remind me of promises I've made or tasks I've put off that need to be done—today. But what he calls me to do he also equips me to do (1 Cor. 1:7). He *never* asks me to do the impossible.

As I'm learning to be obedient—to be a doer of his Word rather than a procrastinator—exciting things are happening. I'm discovering the joy of being used in his kingdom work in ways I could have easily missed. Just as God made Eric Liddell (of *Chariots of Fire* fame) a runner, God made me a writer. And I feel his pleasure when I write!

~✎

RESPONDING TO GOD'S CALL TO WRITE

Ecclesiastes 3:1 says, "There is a right time for everything." This may not be the right time for you to write. But if you have clearly felt God's call to write and you know you are procrastinating, you need to pray, "Cross-examine me, O Lord, . . . test my motives and affections too" (Ps. 26:2). Remembering that God "deserve[s] honesty from the heart; yes, utter sincerity and truthfulness" (Ps. 51:6), answer the following questions.

Why do I procrastinate?

What ideas have I scribbled on a scrap of paper that I know I should be developing?

If I knew Jesus was coming back this week, or this month, or this year, what completed manuscript would I most want to lay at his feet?

10

First Things First

Give him first place in your life
and live as he wants you to.
MATTHEW 6:33

"Oh no!" I wailed as my blurry eyes read the time on the clock. "The alarm didn't go off!"

I scrambled out of bed and rushed downstairs to throw breakfast together and pack lunches. "Hurry up!" I shouted.

I felt as though I was always racing—and losing. No matter how often I reminded myself that there were enough hours to do what God wanted me to do, I often suffered from tension headaches.

"Analyzing the situation won't help," I told myself as I sank into a chair after pushing everyone out the door. Clutter greeted me everywhere I looked. Crumpled homework papers, crayons, toys, dirty socks. My husband didn't mind the way the house looked, but I did. It was a reflection of me! I resented my children for being so sloppy and accused myself of failing as a homemaker and mother.

My thoughts wandered to the writing assignment waiting for me in my bedroom/office. There were letters I'd put off answering and new ideas begging to be developed. My files desperately needed cleaning to make room for the piles on my floor and desk. And I was behind in bookkeeping.

"Oh God!" I cried as I buried my face in my hands. "Why can't I ever get on top of things? I feel so defeated."

"First things first," the Lord spoke gently to my spirit.

I felt certain my goals lined up with God's will for my life. The problem came in trying to break them into specific and manageable tasks and not allowing them to be pushed aside by other pressures. Mark Porter says, "The tyranny of the urgent frustrates every goal we hold sacred. . . . The difference between the disorganized person on the edge of a breakdown and the calm, unflappable type is often that the second has determined what is important. He does not waste time, anxiety, or energy on the unimportant"(*The Time of Your Life,* Wheaton, IL: Victor, 1983, p. 173).

"But Lord, what do I do when it all seems important—when I'm being pulled in so many directions by people and things that demand my time?"

I have to admit I've not found an easy answer to this question. Determining and doing those "first things first" is something I struggle with daily. The process, however, is teaching me some important lessons.

First of all, I need to constantly recognize and affirm that while writing is my work, "I can do it only because Christ's mighty energy is at work within me" (Col. 1:29). This means the *first* thing is time to connect with him in prayer and Bible study. I'm reminded how Martin Luther said that the more he had to do, the more time he spent in prayer.

I need to stay close to Jesus and learn how he dealt with pressure (Heb. 12:2). He promised peace of heart and mind—a peace that is *not* contingent on the length of my to-do list (John 14:27). I need to claim his promise as well as remember the condition that goes with the promise in Isaiah 26:3: "He will keep in perfect peace all those who trust in him, whose thoughts turn often to the Lord!"

I also need to be constantly on guard against the Evil One (1 Pet. 5:8). He knows where and when I am most vulnerable. When disappointment and discouragement have not caused me to give up, he simply tries another tactic. Getting me uptight about time pressures is one of his frequent strategies.

Finally I need to discern what everything is from God's point of view. It's not everything I think I have to do! It's not being everything to everybody! It's learning to say no. It's teaching my children to be more responsible. It's time blocking my days so I do not push aside the "first things first" which God says should take priority.

My struggle to do first things first can be exhausting. "But they that wait upon the Lord shall renew their strength. They shall mount up with wings like eagles; they shall run and not be weary; they shall walk and not faint" (Isa. 40:31).

PRESSURES

Father, I have so much to do
and not enough hours in the day to do it.
I know that's only partly true.
I do have enough time
to do the things you want me to do.
But, Lord, how do I sort out what they are,
when everything screams for my attention?
I'm exhausted from rushing—
uptight and irritable.
Please forgive me and help me.
Help me to learn from your Son.
People were constantly pressing in on him.
He could have been consumed—burned out.
But Jesus took time to be alone with you.
He made you his top priority.
I must learn to do the same,
especially when I'm feeling pressured.
Help me to be still and know
that you are God.
Even as you created and hold together the universe,
you can bring order to my life if I will let you.
Thank you, Lord.

~⊘

RESPONDING TO GOD'S CALL TO WRITE

The Lord is teaching me to "pappcott" my pressures. Do a topical study of the key words in this acrostic, adding other Scriptures that God brings to your attention.

Pray—*1 Peter 5:7; Philippians 4:6-7*

Attitude—*Philippians 2:5*

Plan—*Proverbs 16:9*

Prioritize—*Proverbs 3:6; 4:7*

Commit—*Psalm 37:5; Proverbs 16:3*

Trust—*1 Corinthians 1:7; Proverbs 3:5*

Thank—*Psalm 7:17*

11

Going and Growing through the Hurts

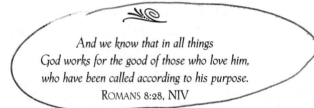

And we know that in all things
God works for the good of those who love him,
who have been called according to his purpose.
ROMANS 8:28, NIV

Have you ever seen the illustration of the zebra whose stripes are unraveling? The caption says, "I think I'm having stress!"

It always gets a good laugh, although I know—from firsthand experience—that stress is anything but a laughing matter. You can't identify because you have a problem-free life? Then, as I tell the folks who attend my writing seminars, you probably haven't suffered enough to be a good writer.

Ouch! That's *not* what you want to hear. But Jesus never promised it would be easy to follow him. While I do not believe he sends stress into our lives, I am convinced that he allows it. Fire is the only way that our faith, which "is far more precious to God than mere gold," is refined and purified (1 Pet. 1:7).

How can you go and grow through the hurts in your own life? Here are some things God has been teaching me—again.

Don't distance yourself from the Lord. It may sound like a cliché, but it's true. If God seems distant, he's not the one who has moved. By an act of our wills, we need to keep drawing near to the Lord during those times when we may feel almost numb from the problems pressing in on us. (Problems are groupies. They never seem to come singly but rather attack us in mass.)

I remember the summer we had no choice but to put my mother in a nursing home—the one thing I told myself I would *never* do. She was only there a few weeks before I had to give the okay to put her in a mental hospital. (Mom had a dementia similar to Alzheimer's and bipolar disorder.) While we were out of town taking our daughter to college, Mom had a metabolic crisis and was moved to another hospital. Three weeks later, the Lord took her home; and just two weeks after her death, my husband lost his job. While I knew God had not deserted us, some days he felt really distant. I had to remember that feelings are not facts and keep on reaching out to him, even when all I could pray was simply, "Help!"

Refuse to dwell on the negatives *or to live in the land of regrets and if onlys.* Hanging above my computer is a little, wooden ornament that says, "Celebrate the Sonrise." (I need visual reminders!) Fact is, no matter how dark things may seem, we can choose to look for and celebrate the blessings we take for granted. Ears to hear, eyes to see, legs to walk, a voice to speak and sing his praises. Friends, family, church. We may not have all these things, but we can choose not to take for granted what we do have and to "think about all [we] can praise God for and be glad about" (Phil. 4:8).

"Be still *and know that [he is] God"* (Ps. 46:10, NIV). Focus on him—on his greatness, his power, his love. "His peace will keep your thoughts and your hearts quiet and at rest as you trust in Christ Jesus" (Phil. 4:7).

Seek prayer support and *counsel of Christian friends and, if necessary, professionals.* Galatians 6:2 says, "Share each other's troubles and problems, and so obey our Lord's command." Doing so means taking off the masks we wear most of the time. Plus we need to go a step further: "Admit your faults to one another and pray for each other so you may be healed" (James 5:16). In the process, not only will we find God's healing but our own problems will seem less overwhelming as we reach out to others.

Search for the truth *that will set you free* (John 8:32). So often we listen to the wrong words as my friend Sue Cameron so powerfully points out in her poem on page 58. We believe the Evil One's accusations and accept his condemnation despite the fact that the Bible says "there is now no condemnation for those who are in Christ Jesus" (Rom. 8:1, NIV).

A year after my mother's homegoing, the Lord clearly showed me that if I continued to beat myself up for the ways *I* felt I had failed her, it was as if I were saying his death on the cross wasn't enough. Truth is that "he is a mighty Savior. He will give you victory. He will rejoice over you in great gladness; he will love you and not accuse you" (Zeph. 3:17-18).

Hang on to his promises. All things *do* work together for good although we may not see how this side of eternity. We can, however, rely on the promise that "he heals the brokenhearted, binding up their wounds" (Ps. 147:3). But just as it takes time for the body to heal when it has been injured, so, too, it takes time for battered emotions to heal. Don't deny the reality of your pain. It's okay to cry. That's why God gave us tears. And remember, "Even when we are too weak to have any faith left, he remains faithful to us and will help us" (2 Tim. 2:13).

Ask, "Lord what are you trying to teach me?"; then share what you learn with others. God does not waste pain and suffering. Instead, he uses it to mold us into the image of his Son and to teach us lessons we would probably learn no other way. He "wonderfully comforts and strengthens us in our hardships and trials. And why does he do this? So that when others are troubled, needing our sympathy and encouragement, we can pass on to them this same help and comfort God has given us" (2 Cor. 1:3-4). That's a promise we can cling to and act on. He is a redeeming God!

RESPONDING TO GOD'S CALL TO WRITE

Read Psalm 40; Romans 5:3-5; and James 1:2-4. What do these passages say to you about God's help to go and grow through your hurts and use them for good?

Words
by Sue Cameron

Is there anything more powerful?
To heal, to hurt,
to destroy?
Words in my mind—accusing me,
dragging me down
into guilt and helplessness.
Words from outside—attacking me,
tearing at the fragile image of who I am and hope to be.
I struggle under their heavy weight
and fear I'll suffocate.
Not all words are true, but they feel true.
Some are lies wrought in the basement of hell,
sent to defeat those who march in the army of God.
My Leader warned me of such warfare,
so subtle and hard to detect.
A sudden attack strips my defenses.
Wounded, bleeding,
I am left to die.
Now my fate depends on
to whom I choose to listen.
To the liar,
or to my Leader.
His Word consoles and strengthens me,
binding my pain and wrapping me in acceptance.
He does not condemn me in my weakness,
or require me to run on broken legs.
He asks only that I listen to him
and believe what he says.
His truth banishes falsehoods
and sets me free.
Living on the battlefield isn't kind and gentle;
it is demanding and stretching.
I must often pause and ask myself,
To whose voice do I listen?
And in whose voice do I speak?

12

Put on the Armor

> Put on the full armor of God
> so that you can take your stand against the devil's schemes.
> For our struggle is not against flesh and blood.
>
> EPHESIANS 6:11-12, NIV

My hands tied behind my back, I was dragged before a tribunal of cloaked men. They accused me of subversion against the government because of my faith in Jesus Christ. I could not deny the charges, for spread across the table were books and articles I had written.

The congregation's singing brought me back to reality. Had I dozed off or seen a vision? I'll never know for sure. But I do know the Lord spoke to me. "Do you realize, Child," I felt him say, "that the things you are writing may one day convict you? Are you willing to follow me despite the cost?"

I didn't answer quickly or feel very brave when I finally said, "Yes, Lord."

That was fifteen years ago. Societally, things were bad and getting worse; but Christians generally were seen as part of the answer—not the problem. We were not the frequent brunt of jokes on TV sitcoms and talk shows. Media coverage was not openly biased. Gays were not militant. People did not worry about being politically correct. The New Age was beginning to infiltrate some churches, but few discerned its danger.

Things are changing—rapidly. We can no longer ignore all the signs that point to the return of Christ. They challenge us to be actively involved in spreading the Gospel while the doors remain open to produce and distribute Christian literature. But we do need to count the cost. In a very real way, writing for the Lord puts us on the front lines where "our struggle is not against flesh and blood, but against the rulers, against the authorities, against the powers of this dark world and against the spiritual forces of evil in the heavenly realms" (Eph. 6:12, NIV). To go into battle without the full armor of God is dangerous.

"This is for keeps, a life-or-death fight to the finish against the Devil and all his angels," *The Message* says. "Be prepared. You're up against far more than you can handle on your own. Take all the help you can get, every weapon God has issued" (Eph. 6:12-13). Having been defeated too often, I'm learning to pray on the armor every morning that I might "resist the enemy whenever he attacks, and when it is all over [I] will still be standing up" (Eph. 6:13).

"Lord," I pray, "help me gird myself with your belt of truth. Give me discernment that I might immediately recognize the enemy's lies and half-truths. Help me to refuse to receive or believe them." When a manuscript is returned and those insistent inner whispers threaten to defeat me, I buckle the belt of God's truth more tightly around me. I affirm, often out loud, that the return of one manuscript (or dozens) does not mean I should quit writing. I know God has called me to write, but that call is not a guarantee of accepted manuscripts. I must keep developing the gifts of writing and marketing and persevere.

The breastplate of righteousness protects my most vulnerable area—my heart, the home of my feelings and emotions. It is so easy for me to be wounded by others, to allow myself to be influenced by fear of what they might say or think. I need to be constantly vigilant against the temptation to compromise because "everyone else is doing it." I cannot pad my writing expenses on Schedule C. I cannot be careless attributing quotes or use copyright material without permission. Instead, I must handle every aspect of the business side of my writing in a way that honors the Lord. My first priority must be to bring glory to him and not to myself. "Lord," I pray, "help me today to consistently choose to do what is right in your eyes."

Putting on the shoes of readiness to share the Gospel protects me from the temptation to get sidetracked. There are often other things I can do and write that would require less time and effort, but if I am to be a soldier of the King, I must take my orders from him. I need to follow his marching orders instead of asking him to bless mine. When I walk in obedience, I find that my feet do not become bruised and weary from going places he never intended me to go. I also find that when I say yes to what he wants me to do, rather than yes to what others tell me I should do or what I feel they expect me to do, I am filled with peace instead of tension.

I prayerfully pick up the shield of faith to "extinguish all the flaming arrows of the evil one" (Eph. 6:16, NIV). I ask God to make me mighty in spirit—to help me walk by faith, not by sight. I also ask him to help me not to lower my shield by nurturing doubts. A soldier can be fatally wounded if he lowers his shield for only a moment.

The helmet of salvation protects my thought life. Each morning I thank God that I do not have to be bound by old habits and thinking patterns. I ask him to continue his work of transforming me by renewing my mind (Rom. 12:2) and giving me the "thoughts and mind of Christ" (1 Cor. 2:16).

Finally, there is the one offensive piece of armor. It is with the "sword of the Spirit, which is the word of God" (Eph. 6:17, NIV) that we go forth into battle to confront the evil of our day. Doing so doesn't mean we are supposed to hit our readers over the head with the Bible. Instead, I pray that God's Word will so permeate my life that the principles of Scripture will be evident in all I do, say, and write.

"The enemy is within the gates," Chuck Colson writes in *Against the Night* (Ann Arbor, MI: Servant, 1989, p. 19). "I believe that we do face a crisis in Western culture, and that it presents the greatest threat to civilization since the barbarians invaded Rome" (p. 23). But God commands us to trust him. Even when facing the "spirit of the antichrist," we need not fear "because the one who is in [us] is greater than the one who is in the world" (1 John 4:3-4, NIV). We need to "pray all the time" (Eph. 6:18) and "be strong in the Lord and in his mighty power" (Eph. 6:10, NIV) knowing that Jesus has already won the battle.

Responding to God's Call to Write

Study Ephesians 6:10-18 in several translations or paraphrases. Ask the Lord to show you what each piece of the armor can mean in your life. List those insights below, and begin to daily pray on the armor.

Belt of truth:

Breastplate of righteousness:

Shoes of readiness:

Shield of faith:

Helmet of salvation:

Sword of the Spirit:

13

Disappointed but Not Discouraged

*Because the Lord God helps me,
I will not be dismayed.*
ISAIAH 50:7

Six rejection slips in one day! It isn't the first time, and I know it won't be the last. I handle them better now than I did when I was a beginning writer, yet they still hurt.

My writing is so much a part of me. It's hard not to view the return of a manuscript as a personal rejection, especially when I've written out of the crucible of my life experience. It's hard not to question the Lord. I seek his help as I write. I invest time, energy, and hard work. I know if I don't do something quickly, disappointment will again turn to discouragement and pull me under.

Then I feel God speak to me through his Word: "Since future victory is sure, be strong and steady, always abounding in the Lord's work, for you know that nothing you do for the Lord is ever wasted as it would be if there were no resurrection" (1 Cor. 15:58).

My thoughts turn to Jesus. "He was willing to die a shameful death on the cross because of the joy he knew would be his afterwards." He wants to be my "leader and instructor" (Heb. 12:2). As the poster over my computer says, "The answer lies in Christ."

I think of the disappointments Jesus faced. The poignancy of the opening lines of John's Gospel again stir me. "Even in his own land and among his own people, the Jews, he was not accepted. Only a few would welcome and receive him" (John 1:11).

Jesus knew firsthand the pain of rejection! He was misunderstood and ridiculed even by his own brothers (John 7:2-5). He endured the criticism of the religious leaders (i.e., John 7:15) and the ostracism of those who felt nothing good could come from Nazareth (John 1:46). And even in Nazareth, those who had known him since childhood refused to believe in him. Mark 6:6 says, "And he could hardly accept the fact that they wouldn't believe in him."

Jesus must have been deeply disappointed at that point in his ministry when "many of his disciples turned away and deserted him" (John 6:66). I can only imagine how he must have felt as he turned to his disciples and asked, "Are you going too?" (John 6:67). I wonder if the others nodded in agreement when Peter said, "Master, to whom shall we go? You alone have the words that give eternal life, and we believe them and know you are the holy Son of God" (John 6:68-69). Or I wonder if some of them harbored unspoken doubts—especially as Jesus began to speak more and more of his death? One thing is certain: Jesus knew their thoughts. He knew Peter would deny him, Judas would betray him, and all of them would desert him.

"Father, strengthen me," I can imagine Jesus praying. "Help me rise above my feelings. Don't let the pain and disappointment I feel cause me to give up the work you have sent me to do. Don't let me give in to discouragement."

While, of course, I do not know what Jesus prayed, I have no doubt that it was through those times alone with his Father that he received the strength he needed to overcome disappointments that make mine seem small in comparison. I also have no doubt that Jesus was a realist. He didn't set himself up for disappointment by putting his trust in men "for he knew mankind to the core. No one needed to tell him how changeable human nature is!" (John 2:24-25).

I believe the parable of the sower (Luke 8:5-15) is Jesus' statement of faith and purpose. He is the Sower, the one who chose to come to earth and spread the seed that yields eternal life for all who believe. Like the farmer who works hard with no guarantee of a bounteous harvest, Jesus knows that not all of the seed sown will take root and grow to maturity. Some seed falls on hard soil, on indifferent hearts. Because they do not allow his Word to penetrate their hearts, Satan is able to snatch it away. Other seed falls on rocky soil, on those whose lives have little spiritual depth. They follow only as long as it is the easy thing to do. Still other seed falls on thorny ground, on those who are more interested in the things of the world than in seeking first his kingdom. But some seed falls on good soil. It takes root and produces a plentiful harvest that is worth the price of death on the cross.

I can hear Jesus speaking to me through this parable. "Be realistic. You can't expect, even with my help, to sell everything you write—certainly not the first time out. Maybe not even the tenth! It takes time and experience to learn to sow your seed effectively. It takes patience to wait while it grows to maturity. It takes faith to learn how to handle disappointment and not become discouraged. These lessons cannot be sidestepped if you want a writing ministry."

And I can also hear Jesus' words of warning. I cannot allow disappointments to beat me down so I become like the hard soil. If I do, the Evil One will be waiting to snatch away my joy and enthusiasm. I cannot become like the stony ground, someone who enjoys going to writers' conferences and being challenged to write but fails to go home and do it. Instead, I must make the decision to be productive by deliberately choosing to let my roots "grow down into him and draw up nourishment from him" (Col. 2:7).

I must be willing to pull out all the thorns, all those things that would distract me from wholeheartedly pursuing my call to write. And I must trust that in God's perfect timing, his words, which have taken root in me, will be put onto paper and published. Even if they are *never* published, he will use them for his kingdom purposes. My life and writing will produce a large crop of fruit if I hear the Word, retain it, and persevere (Luke 8:15).

RESPONDING TO GOD'S CALL TO WRITE

Read one of the Gospels, making a list of situations that could have caused Jesus to feel disappointed and discouraged. Note how he handled each situation. Apply what you learn to your own life, keeping a journal of your experiences so you can later use them as grist for your writing mill.

One of the best ways to deal with disappointments is to get your eyes off yourself and onto someone else—especially onto the hopes, goals, and needs of another writer. Do you know someone who shows promise as a writer, someone who could or should be writing? Do you know a beginning writer you can nurture or a struggling writer you can encourage? Write that person's name below, and begin to pray for her or him. Ask God to show you how he wants you to reach out to this person.

No Other Way

But Father,
is there no other way?
I can go to the cross,
yet there is no guarantee
my sacrifice will make any difference.
Even though I pay the price for sin
and offer the gift of eternal life,
men are reticent to change.
They may reject the gift I offer.
I may suffer in vain.
And yet, Father, if there is but one
who will come to you
as a result of my shed blood . . .
Father, I give myself to your plan
for the redemption of mankind.

14

Me—A Servant?

*I became a servant of this gospel
by the gift of God's grace
given me through the working of his power.*
EPHESIANS 3:7, NIV

"Who do you think I am, your servant?" my mother would complain when I'd leave my things lying around.

I'd roll my eyes. "You should be happy I'm not as sloppy as most of my girlfriends."

"Teenagers," she'd grumble and throw up her hands in dismay. "When will you ever learn?"

The learning started when I got married! Why couldn't my husband put his dirty clothes in the hamper? That was just as easy as throwing them on the floor. "I didn't marry you to be your servant," I'd complain.

And then the kids came along and began scattering their stuff from one end of the house to the other. I have especially painful memories of stepping on Rob's Lego™ toys. Now the roles were reversed. Daily I gave my kids the same lecture my mom used to give me.

Who's in charge? Who's the servant? It's an ongoing conflict in most homes, places of business, and even churches.

The night before Jesus went to the cross, he got up from the table, wrapped a towel around his waist, and one by one began

washing his disciples' feet. Considering the arguments the disciples
had about who would be greatest in the kingdom, it was an important and graphic lesson. To make sure they "got it," Jesus explained,
"I have given you an example to follow: do as I have done to you"
(John 13:15).

"Among you it is different," he told them another time when
the rest of the Twelve learned of the request James and John had
made to sit on thrones next to his. "Whoever wants to be great
among you must be your servant. And whoever wants to be greatest of all must be the slave of all. For even I, the Messiah, am not
here to be served, but to help others, and to give my life as a ransom
for many" (Mark 10:43-45).

I'm certain it was *not* what they wanted to hear. I can imagine
them thinking, "Haven't you maybe, hopefully, got that reversed?"

God says, "My thoughts are not your thoughts, neither are
your ways my ways" (Isa. 55:8, NIV). How true! In fact, much of the
time what God asks us to do is totally the opposite of our human
nature.

How can we become the servant he is calling us to be? Here are
four steps to take.

Rely on his life-transforming power. When Rob was a little
boy and I used to ask him to clean up his room, he'd moan and
groan over what, to him, seemed to be an impossible task. So, too,
we may conclude it is impossible to live as God's servant in a society that programs us, almost from birth, to get what we want *when*
we want it. Although Jesus willingly "laid aside his mighty power
and glory, taking the disguise of a slave" (Phil. 2:7), in our human
nature we'd prefer not to be a servant, thank you very much.

How do we change? We can't! As the apostle Paul discovered,
we become servants of this Gospel "by the gift of God's grace given
[us] through the working of his power" (Eph. 3:7, NIV). While few
of us will have a Damascus Road experience, we each need to surrender our desires to be served in order that we may serve him and
others.

Ask, "What would Jesus do?" This question was the premise of
Charles Sheldon's classic work, *In His Steps*. Today, through a variety of Christian products, it's become the "in" question to ask. It's
certainly a question that fits the servanthood Jesus exemplified: "For

these are not my own ideas, but I have told you what the Father said to tell you" (John 12:49). He couldn't have made it any clearer.

Do we consistently ask, "What would Jesus do?" When we sit in front of our computers and seek to write his answer, do we listen for the guidance he will give us?

Allow yourself to be taught. Years ago every carpenter, bricklayer, printer, and workman of most any kind was likely to have one or more apprentices. Hour by hour, day by day, the master craftsman taught his trade to his pupil. By watching and imitating, the apprentice learned in a hands-on way what could never be learned from a book.

Christians who want to become excellent writers also need to serve an apprentice relationship with an experienced wordsmith. Ask the Lord to send someone alongside who is both a mature Christian and a gifted writer. Put yourself into an accountability relationship with him or her. And then, as you grow spiritually and professionally, pass along the same gift to another believer who wants to serve God through the ministry of writing.

Choose to be a good servant. Because God has given us free wills, the Bible has many examples of good and bad servants. Bad servants lie, steal, and covet. They are quarrelsome and more interested in pleasing men than God. They are deceitful and unmerciful and will not submit to correction.

And what of good servants? They choose to be wise, faithful, and obedient to their masters. They put the master's will first. "They delight in doing everything God wants them to, and day and night are always meditating on his laws and thinking about ways to follow him more closely" (Ps. 1:2).

Being a servant of the Word is an awesome and serious responsibility. With it comes greater accountability: "We who teach will be judged more strictly" (James 3:1, NIV).

~⊛~

RESPONDING TO GOD'S CALL TO WRITE

Do a topical study of the words *serve* and *servant.* Then read the following two parables Jesus told about servants. What is he saying to you about your calling as a servant of the Word? Record his answers below.

Matthew 24:45-51

Matthew 25:14-30

SERVANTS OF THE WORD
by Mary Nixon

Lord, grant that your servants
with confidence speak,
your Word so that broken hearts mend.
Please lead them to your light,
let them hear what we write,
and show them your love never ends.

Servants of the Word are we,
proclaiming your truth throughout eternity.
We lift up our voice,
and praise you, rejoice!
Servants of the Word are we.

Lord, help us to write
the words that will win,
all those who are lost in their sin.
May our spirits be bright,
as we bring them your light,
that shines to the world from within.

In Dry Times

"I'll never run out of ideas," I've often said. With a file drawer full of notes and manuscripts in various stages of completion, I felt certain that periods of dryness, or writer's block, which I heard other writers complain about, would not affect me. But then something happened that was far worse. I felt empty inside!

The Evil One began to fill me with doubts. "You so often fail to live as a Christian," he whispered in my ear. "How can you expect to help others? You're nothing but a hypocrite. You have no business trying to be a writer."

Every time I sat down at my desk, I got a tension headache. Increasingly I began to dread facing the work I had always loved to do. "Maybe it is time to quit," I said to my husband one evening. "I'm willing to work hard and face rejection, but if I don't have anything to share. . . "

Paul put his arms around me. "You'll feel inspired again. I know you will."

"But what if God doesn't want me to write anymore?"

The phone rang. It was an editor asking me to write a series of devotionals. My heart pounded with excitement. An assignment on a Sunday evening from an editor, right after I had questioned my call. It couldn't be a coincidence! I thanked God for showing me that my writing ministry wasn't over.

With new enthusiasm I sat down at my typewriter the next morning, but still I felt empty. Ideas wouldn't flow. I turned to the discouraging task of resubmitting manuscripts. As I plodded along, the whispers grew more intense. "You're a failure. You don't have what it takes. God can't use you."

I couldn't get to sleep that night. I tried praying, but God seemed distant. Suddenly I remembered something Lee Roddy told me when I was struggling to complete my first book. "You're listening to the wrong voice, Marlene," he said.

The burden began to lift as I thought of Lee's words and the Scriptures that point to Satan as the father of lies. He is the Christian writer's great adversary. He is intent on destroying our writing ministries, our homes, our lives.

"But God," I prayed, "it's sometimes so hard to discern your voice. The enemy's whispers seem so true. I *do* fail to respond to situations in Christlike ways—to practice what I preach. It's easy to believe those failures make me unworthy to share your Word."

"Condemnation is the work of the Evil One," God reminded me. "My Spirit brings conviction of sin and the strength to overcome him. I know you're not perfect. None of the people I use are perfect. They are willing people. Are you still willing, Child?"

"Oh yes, Lord," I said as I fervently prayed I would again experience the anointing of his Spirit. "Please speak to me so that I can write the words you want me to write."

The next day my writer's block lifted. Sentences began to flow—not in perfect form or structure—but then that never has been my experience. I always spend a lot of time rewriting and editing. But, praise God, I again had words to rewrite and edit!

Since then I've experienced other times of dryness. They seem almost cyclical, like the droughts that periodically occur in nature. I know God allows these times in my life to teach me valuable lessons about the importance of letting my roots grow down into him (Col. 2:7). And so, I endeavor to follow his drought emergency instructions in James 4:6-10:

1. Humble yourself before the Lord and ask him to remove any false pride (v. 6). Affirm anew that he is the Source of your creativity.

2. "Submit yourselves, then, to God" (v. 7, NIV). *The NIV Interlinear Greek-English New Testament* reads: "Be ye subject therefore to God." The Greek word for "subject," *hupotasso,* is "primarily a military term, to rank under" according to *Vine's Expository Dictionary of New Testament Words.* We need to remember that God is not our buddy or our errand boy. Rather, "all things were created by him and for him. He is before all things, and in him all things hold together. And he is the head of the body, the church" (Col. 1:16-18, NIV).

3. "Resist the devil" (v. 7, NIV). Put on the helmet of salvation (Eph. 6:17) to protect your mind from the Evil One's accusations. Pick up the shield of faith to "extinguish all the flaming arrows of the evil one" (Eph. 6:16, NIV).

4. "Come near to God" (v. 8, NIV). Whether you feel his presence or not, spend an increased amount of time in prayer and in his Word. To stop your mind from wandering, pray aloud or write down your prayers. You might also want to read Scripture aloud. Grab hold of the promise: "Forever, O Lord, your Word stands firm in heaven. Your faithfulness extends to every generation, like the earth you created; it endures by your decree, for everything serves your plans" (Ps. 119:89-91).

5. "Grieve, mourn and wail" (v. 9, NIV) over the ways you fail the Lord. Ask him to make you a cleansed vessel through which his power can flow.

6. "Realize your worthlessness before the Lord" and allow him to "lift you up, encourage and help you" (v. 10).

I praise God for the way "he lifted me out of the pit of despair, out from the bog and the mire, and set my feet on a hard, firm path and steadied me as I walked along. He has given me a new song to sing, of praises to our God. Now many will hear of the glorious things he did for me, and stand in awe before the Lord, and put their trust in him" (Ps. 40:2-3).

RESPONDING TO GOD'S CALL TO WRITE

Expand on the drought emergency instructions by using a concordance to find additional Scriptures for these key words and phrases:

Humility

Submission

Resist the Evil One

Draw near to God

Repentance

Forgiveness

16

Be Honest

I am still not all I should be.
PHILIPPIANS 3:13

"Write about what you know." We've heard it over and over, but it's true. Our strongest writing is likely to grow out of our personal experiences. That's *not* to say, however, that all writers are called to write personal experience stories or their salvation testimonies, but if you feel you are, this chapter is for you.

Reading through Acts and Paul's letters, it's obvious he felt called to write from personal experience. To do so effectively, he knew he needed to be open, honest, and vulnerable.

"I am still not all I should be," Paul admitted to the Christians in Philippi (Phil. 3:13). How important it is confess this truth to God and ourselves. "Create in me a clean heart, O God," we need to pray (Ps. 51:10, KJV). Only then can we be cleansed vessels through which his Spirit can flow to teach others his ways (Ps. 51:13).

Recognizing how far short we fall from God's glory (Rom. 3:23) reminds us to approach our readers with humility, rather than a know-it-all, I've arrived attitude. Being open and honest about our own struggles and failures creates that all-important reader identification without which people won't read beyond the first paragraph.

How open and honest do we need to be? Do we have to tell our readers everything? No! Not only would we bore them, but if we are writing our salvation testimonies, we might end up glorifying sin instead of the Savior. Wisdom says to carefully and prayerfully discern how much God wants us to share. We then need to stay within the boundaries he sets, sharing no more and no less.

According to Acts 8:3, before his conversion, "Paul was like a wild man, going everywhere to devastate the believers, even entering private homes and dragging out men and women alike and jailing them." Even though Paul knew the Lord had forgiven him, it still must have grieved him to remember the pain he inflicted on those who were now fellow believers.

For years, Paul chafed under the distrust of the church leaders. Despite the later success of his missionary tours and all the suffering he endured for the cause of Christ, he was never totally accepted by some of the Jewish believers.

It would have been natural and understandable for Paul to want to forget his past and even to try and hide it. Instead, before a mob at the temple in Jerusalem, Paul admitted he "persecuted the Christians, hounding them to death, binding and delivering both men and women to prison" (Acts 22:4). But then he went on to describe how the Lord met him on the road to Damascus and dramatically changed his life: "Even though I was once a blasphemer and a persecutor and a violent man," Paul later wrote to Timothy, "I was shown mercy because I acted in ignorance and unbelief. . . . Christ Jesus came into the world to save sinners—of whom I am the worst. But for that very reason I was shown mercy so that in me, the worst of sinners, Christ Jesus might display his unlimited patience as an example for those who would believe on him and receive eternal life" (1 Tim. 1:13, 15-16, NIV).

We, too, have the opportunity to share our witness of the ways Christ has changed us with those who may feel there is no hope for them. By taking off our masks and being real, we can "shine out among them like beacon lights, holding out to them the Word of Life" (Phil. 2:15).

Again, we can learn from Paul's example of honesty and openness. He admitted he didn't understand himself. "I really want to do what is right," he wrote, "but I can't. I do what I don't want to—

what I hate" (Rom. 7:15). Yet out of his awareness of his own sinful nature, Paul was able to point others to "the power of the life-giving Spirit" (Rom. 8:2). We can do the same.

But what about the Evil One's accusation that we have no business writing our testimonies because we're not always living in victory? Once again we need to look to Paul. From prison in Rome he wrote to the Philippians: "I haven't learned all I should even yet, but I keep working toward that day when I will finally be all that Christ saved me for and wants me to be" (Phil. 3:12). It is not our goodness or our obedience to God's laws that will save us or our readers; rather, it is the shed blood of Jesus Christ. We need to point our readers to the Cross, not to ourselves.

Finally, Paul realistically portrayed the difficulties involved in following Christ: "We are pressed on every side by troubles," he wrote, "but not crushed and broken. We are perplexed because we don't know why things happen as they do, but we don't give up and quit. We are hunted down, but God never abandons us. We get knocked down, but we get up again and keep going" (2 Cor. 4:8-9).

Paul's call to spread the Good News of Jesus Christ to the Gentile world was not an easy one. He patiently endured "suffering and hardship and trouble of every kind" (2 Cor. 6:4), but these were the very things that made his words credible. He was able to *show* from his personal experience how God would also "tenderly comfort" his readers and give them the "strength to endure" (2 Cor. 1:6-7).

Just as Paul urged the early Christians to pattern their lives after his (Phil. 3:17), I believe he would urge those of us who are called to minister through personal experience stories and testimonies to pattern our writing after his. With God's help we can, like Paul, write openly and honestly in such a way that unbelievers will be won to Christ and believers will be encouraged and strengthened.

~~∿◎~~

RESPONDING TO GOD'S CALL TO WRITE

If you are not called to write personal experience stories or your salvation testimony, please don't assume a burden of false guilt. God gives us gifts that differ! See chapter 29, "Finding Our Place," and know that the type of writing God has called you to do is what best fits the uniqueness of who he has created you to be. Study the Scriptures in "Writing Your Testimony," page 153; and consider what it means to be open, honest, and vulnerable in the writing he is calling you to do.

If you are called to write personal experience stories, inventory the rough moments of your life. When were you most aware of God's presence? When did you grow the most? List two or three experiences below.

Bring your list to the Lord and ask him for direction. Is he calling you to write one of these stories now or to wait? Remember, there's a big difference between writing for your readers and writing as therapy.

Study the Scriptures and do's and don'ts in "Writing Your Testimony," page 153. Write a testimony of what God has done in your life, being careful not to set yourself up as the model or norm of what others should experience.

17

Bearing Fruit

~~✿~~

*"I chose you and appointed you
to go and bear fruit."*
JOHN 15:16, NIV

It is a bitter cold February day. As I sit at my computer and look out the window, I can't help but daydream. A winter storm has encrusted the trees and bushes with a thick layer of ice that glistens in the bright sunshine. Spring seems a long way off. Wistfully I dream of golden daffodils and fragrant lilacs.

My thoughts wander to the vegetable seeds I planted yesterday in window boxes on my toasty radiator. Although they are weeks from sprouting, I'm already thinking how good it will be to have fresh, homegrown tomatoes, peppers, and cauliflower. The ringing of the phone brings me back to the present and, after a brief conversation, back to this blank screen. "Lord, what do you want to say through me?" I ask.

"Bear fruit," I feel him speak to my heart.

I sigh. For all my hard work this past month, I don't feel I have borne much fruit. January's mail was slow to bring acceptances or checks.

"I feel as if I've plowed and planted my garden, but nothing is growing," I complain. "It's not that I mind the hard work, Lord. But when am I going to see the fruit of my labors?"

"Have you forgotten what I taught you about abiding?"

I open my Bible to John 15:4 and read: "Take care to live in me, and let me live in you. For a branch can't produce fruit when severed from the vine. Nor can you be fruitful apart from me."

I think back over the past weeks and the many excuses I've made to shortchange my quiet time with the Lord. It's no wonder my writing is not bearing fruit. I have been trying to do it in my strength instead of his.

Again the Lord reminds me that my relationship with him is more important than anything I can do for him. Then, in a new way, I also see the kind of fruit he longs for me to bear. Far more important than powerful prose or beautiful poetry is the fruit of Christlikeness.

"But when the Holy Spirit controls our lives he will produce this kind of fruit in us: love, joy, peace, patience, kindness, goodness, faithfulness, gentleness and self-control," I read from Galatians 5:22-23. I have to admit that sometimes this fruit is sadly lacking in my life.

Love for the Lord and my readers is not always my motivating force. Too often I am caught up in the ego trip of seeing my name in bigger and better magazines. When editors do not accept my work, I do not feel very loving towards them.

My joy is lost when I push myself to get manuscripts in the mail and measure my fruitfulness by the number of acceptances I receive in return. My peace is destroyed when I take my focus off the Lord and put it on myself—on my goals, my needs, my feelings.

My patience wears thin when things don't happen as quickly as I want and feel they should. Instead of waiting on God and his perfect timing, I become discouraged and irritable. I say unkind things to the people I love, especially to my children, when they interrupt me when I'm trying to write.

Goodness makes me think of Paul's words about Jesus: "He went around doing good" (Acts 10:38). Am I "doing good" through what I write? Using Lee Roddy's acrostic, BERT, do my words really Benefit my readers? Do they Enrich them? Are they Relevant and Timely?

Faithfulness. The Bible assures me that "the one who calls [me] is faithful" (1 Thess. 5:24, NIV). Therefore, I do not have to become consumed by the dollars and hours part of my writing—by the little I earn for the long hours I work. Instead, I can choose to trust his promise to supply all my needs (Phil. 4:19) and to remain faithful to my call to write his answer.

Gentleness, I learn as I look at the original Greek meaning of the word, is not just the way I treat others. *The NIV Interlinear Greek-English New Testament* translates it as "meekness." *Vine's Expository Dictionary of New Testament Words* says, "It consists not in a person's 'outward' behaviour only; nor yet in his relations to his fellow-men. . . . It is that temper of spirit in which we accept His dealings with us as good, and therefore without disputing or resisting." In other words, instead of almost demanding that God "bless" my ministry, I must surrender my desires to him. I need to follow Jesus' example and remember how he took on "the very nature of a servant, . . . humbled himself and became obedient to death" (Phil. 2:7-8, NIV).

Self-control makes me think of discipline and my need to take control of the hours in each day, as well as my thoughts, feelings, and actions which often defeat me. I can choose to dwell on the positives and not procrastinate. Most of all, I can choose to relinquish control of my life to the Lord every day and trust him to work in me and through me.

"Yes, I am the Vine; you are the branches," I feel him speak to me again through his Word. "Whoever lives in me and I in him shall produce a large crop of fruit" (John 15:5). He doesn't say when, but he also doesn't say maybe. Instead, he gives me the conditions. I must deliberately choose to abide in him and submit wholeheartedly to his pruning of my motives and goals. I must take care to stay close to him—to let him live in me. Only then will my life and my words bear fruit.

※

RESPONDING TO GOD'S CALL TO WRITE

Prayerfully consider whether or not love, joy, peace, patience, kindness, goodness, faithfulness, gentleness, and self-control are evident in your life. Then read Jeremiah 17:7-8; John 15:1-8; and Galatians 5:22-23, asking the Lord to show you how he wants you to grow in him. Write his answer in the space below.

THE MASTER GARDENER

He planted the seed in the ground.
Ever so slowly it changed—
actually it died—
that it might be reborn into something new.
It began to push through the soil.
First one, then another leaf appeared.
From a spindly little seedling
it kept growing—and changing—
until it became a sturdy, bushy plant.
Buds formed, and then beautiful flowers unfolded.

In our Christian walk,
we too must first die to ourselves,
surrendering our wills to that of our Maker.
The newness of his life within us
begins to germinate
and take root.
We begin to push through problems and obstacles.
As we continue to draw up nourishment from him—
to become strong and vigorous in his truth—
fruit that we could never produce by ourselves
begins to first bud, and then bloom.
And it is all the work of the Master Gardener.

18

Seek First His Kingdom

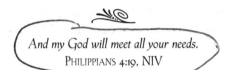

And my God will meet all your needs.
PHILIPPIANS 4:19, NIV

"May the Lord bring a new joy in letting him carry the burden for you so that you do not feel the pressure to perform."

I blink in amazement at the letter from an editor I deeply respect. Her words are incredibly on target. How did she know the financial pressure I have been under and the pressure I feel to "perform" as a writer? I know for certain I haven't said anything to her. I'm not in the habit of sharing my financial needs with editors, even those who are good friends. Yet somehow she looked into my soul and saw the struggle that some days threatens to make me give up.

God has called me to write. Neither I nor my husband question his call. I know Paul fully supports my choice to stay home and write. But I also know our financial obligations make my writing seem like an unaffordable luxury. If I put in the same number of hours at a "real" job, there would be a regular paycheck. I wouldn't need to worry about how we are going to pay for college for our two children or the repairs our house desperately needs. And Paul would not have to work a second job delivering pizzas.*

It is as if I'm engaged in a tug of war between what I know I am supposed to be doing and the realities that make it seem unrealistic.

I feel guilty staying home and writing when I see my children doing without some things I'd like to be able to give them. And then the doubts come. I wonder whether I am torturing myself with writing aspirations that are only pipe dreams.

I'm sure I'm not alone in this struggle. In today's economy, most everyone who seriously pursues a writing ministry has to consider the cost involved. The fact is that it takes more than just time and talent to be a successful writer. There is also the investment of money—for a computer, printer, and software, as well as for postage, supplies, conferences, books, magazines, etc. And there is no guarantee we will recoup our expenses, much less make a profit.

Most Christian writers will claim a loss for several years. Even when we get out of the red, it may be a long time (if ever) before we are making what we could in K Mart. I wonder whether people in other professions are willing to put in the same long hours for the amount of money I earn writing for Christian periodicals.

To be honest, sometimes I feel angry and resentful over the hard work and poor pay. At times the sacrifices seem too great and the rewards too small. Because my writing is also my livelihood (or needs to be), I can't ignore these very real feelings. Instead, I must gain victory over them.

I am reminded of Jesus' words about God and money in the Sermon on the Mount. Jesus knew the hardships his countrymen endured because of the heavy taxes Rome imposed. When crops failed or the nets were empty, no doubt many went hungry. Yet Jesus told them not to worry about food, drink, or clothes. He sought to change their perspective—to help them see that they should be grateful for life itself.

Jesus drew their attention to the birds of the air. "They don't worry about what to eat—they don't need to sow or reap or store up food—for your heavenly Father feeds them. And," he reminded them, "you are far more valuable to him than they are" (Matt. 6:26).

He pointed to the lilies in the field. "King Solomon in all his glory was not clothed as beautifully as they" (Matt. 6:29). Again he spoke words of reassurance. "And if God cares so wonderfully for flowers that are here today and gone tomorrow, won't he more surely care for you, O men of little faith?" (Matt. 6:30).

His words convict me. My faith is little. My perspective is wrong. Although God promises to meet all my needs, I waste a tremendous amount of emotional energy worrying. This gives Satan a dangerous foothold in my life. I allow him to rob me of the joy of writing when I embrace negative thinking patterns and my list of "have nots." As a result, more times than I want to admit, I've wondered if I should just give up. Because my work is not selling and ministering to people? No. Because what I earn from manuscript sales never seems to be enough.

Then something else Jesus said comes to mind. "But seek first his kingdom and his righteousness, and all these things will be given to you as well" (Matt. 6:33, NIV).

That is the key! I must keep my priorities in order—must keep my eyes on the Lord and the kingdom work he is calling me to do. I cannot lose sight of my call by allowing my writing to get tangled up with my worry about our finances. I need to see God as our Source instead of trying to "produce" bigger and better manuscripts that will bring in larger and more frequent checks. I have been assuming a burden God never meant for me to carry instead of trusting him to provide.

"Lord, please forgive me and help me," I pray. "Forgive me for putting a price tag on the work I do for you. Forgive me for my worry and my desire for earthly rewards. Help me to see everything I do in light of eternity."

The sense of release, which my editor friend prayed I would discover, comes as cleansing tears flow down my cheeks. The weight lifts as I give my worries to the Lord and renew my commitment to write his answer.

I know I'll have to do this over and over again. Victory is rarely instantaneous and complete. But I also know I'm going in the right direction because in a new way, I'm seeking first his kingdom and his righteousness regardless of the cost. The other things—my genuine needs—will be taken care of by the Lord in his perfect timing. I can trust him. So can you.

RESPONDING TO GOD'S CALL TO WRITE

God doesn't call everyone to be a full-time writer, but he does call all of us to trust him and walk in obedience. Are you trusting and obeying, or are you thinking "lack"—lack of money, time, ability, or anything else?

Why do you feel this way?

Read Philippians 4:19. Make a list of the needs he has met in your life.

What, specifically, is God asking you to do today to show that you believe this promise?

---

*God has been faithful! My son is in his fourth year of college; my daughter, in her fourth year of medical school. Our house has not fallen down around us. And Paul no longer needs to deliver pizzas!

19

Proclaim Freedom

"He has sent me to proclaim freedom."
LUKE 4:18, NIV

It was the first Independence Day. Rising to his feet in his home-town synagogue, Jesus was handed the book of the prophet Isaiah. He began to read, "The Spirit of the Lord is upon me; he has appointed me to preach Good News to the poor; he has sent me to heal the brokenhearted and to announce that captives shall be released and the blind shall see, that the downtrodden shall be freed from their oppressors, and that God is ready to give blessings to all who come to him" (Luke 4:18-19).

I can imagine how every eye was riveted on him as he added, "These Scriptures came true today!" (Luke 4:21).

There were no fireworks or hurrahs. Instead, people began to whisper among themselves.

"Isn't this Joseph's son?" someone must have asked.

"But he's so eloquent and wise."

"I heard he's been working miracles in Capernaum."

"How can that be? We've known him all his life."

"Yes, who does he think he is?"

"I solemnly declare to you," Jesus said, "that no prophet is accepted in his own home town! For example, remember how

Elijah the prophet used a miracle to help the widow of Zarephath—a foreigner from the land of Sidon. There were many Jewish widows needing help in those days of famine. . . . Or think of the prophet Elisha, who healed Naaman, a Syrian, rather than the many Jewish lepers needing help" (Luke 4:24-27).

His remarks infuriated them. As William Barclay says in his commentary *The Gospel of Luke*, "The Jews were so sure that they were God's people that they utterly despised all others. . . . And here was this young Jesus, whom they all knew, preaching as if the *gentiles* were specially favoured by God" (Louisville, KY: Westminster John Knox Press, 1975, p. 48). They mobbed him and took him to the edge of the hill on which the city was built. They were ready to push him over the cliff, but Jesus freely "walked away through the crowd and left them" (Luke 4:30).

Mark's account says Jesus "could hardly accept the fact that they wouldn't believe in him" (6:6). I can feel his disappointment, but I also feel disappointed for the people of Nazareth. There is no record in the Gospels of Jesus ever returning to Nazareth. What a loss for those people! Because of their unbelief, only a few heard the Good News and experienced the healing, freeing, restoring of sight, lifting of burdens, and blessings that Jesus came to bring.

Just as people had a choice 2,000 years ago, they have a choice today. Christians who write also have a choice. We can accept or reject Jesus' words. We can proclaim the message of freedom that cost Jesus his life, or we can water down the power of the Gospel and the Resurrection.

Water down the Gospel? That would never be our intent! Yet unless we are experiencing firsthand the implications of Jesus' Independence Day proclamation, we will not be as effective as we could be in sharing it with our readers.

We need to ask ourselves if we really understand what Jesus meant by preaching "Good News to the poor." Do we understand the significance of the word *poor*? Do we recognize that without him we are nothing? Do we daily admit our need for him and humbly put our complete trust in him? And do we take time to sit at his feet and learn more about the Good News he wants us to impart? "God was in Christ, restoring the world to himself, no longer counting men's sins against them but blotting them out. This is the wonderful message he has given us to tell others" (2 Cor. 5:19).

Jesus said he came to "heal the brokenhearted." If we are struggling with deep, unresolved hurts or if an unforgiving spirit has caused resentment and bitterness to get a foothold in our lives, then we need to allow God to heal our hearts. He never intended for us to go through life sapped of our energy and joy by experiences—perhaps some as far back as our childhoods—that we could not control and certainly cannot change. He wants to make us whole!

Jesus also said he came to "announce that captives shall be released." *Webster's New Dictionary* defines captive as "a person caught and held prisoner." If we are honest with ourselves, we have to admit we're frequently prisoners to negative thinking patterns, doubts, fears, and feelings of discouragement. Or we may be prisoners to bad habits. Are we asking him to set us free?

With his touch, Jesus healed many who were blind. I suspect that some of them knew more than just the joy of seeing the earth and sky, trees, and people. Undoubtedly, many eyes were opened to spiritual truths they had never seen before. What about us? Are we seeing things clearly, or is our vision blurred? Do we need him to touch us and heal us so we can see life from his perspective?

The first-century Israelites were people downtrodden by their oppressors. The Romans imposed heavy taxes and quickly quenched any flames—or even sparks—of political unrest. Today people are still oppressed by cruel governments and merciless economic systems. On a more personal level, many of us know the oppression of being weighed down by heavy emotional or financial burdens or being persecuted for the stand we take as Christians. Others may experience, in very real ways, the oppression of the Evil One. Are we trusting Jesus to give us victory?

Finally, Jesus proclaimed that God was "ready to give blessings to all who come to him." Again we have to ask ourselves whether we wait long enough in his presence to receive all he has for us. Do we give him prime time each day, or do we squeeze him in only when it is convenient or when our needs are desperate?

Jesus' first Independence Day proclamation is filled with promises for us today. As we claim and act on them, we will find our lives filled with new power. Then when we take up our pens to write, God's truth—the truth that truly does set men free—will resound throughout the land.

RESPONDING TO GOD'S CALL TO WRITE

Prayerfully reflect on Luke 4:18-19, and ask the Lord to show you ways you can more fully experience and write about the following truths.

Good News for the poor

Healing for the brokenhearted

Freedom for the captives

Recovery of sight for the blind

Victory for the downtrodden

God's blessings

20

Stop Complaining

In everything you do, stay away from complaining.
PHILIPPIANS 2:14

Read through the Gospels. Do you find even one instance where Jesus complained? There were times when he sighed over people's hardheartedness and indifference to spiritual things and times when he grew weary of their unwillingness to understand and follow him, but Jesus never complained. Not once in the Bible do we hear him say, "Father, I don't know *why* you sent me to these miserable people! I'm wasting my time. I don't see how you expect me to teach them anything. And these thick-headed disciples you've given me. . . "

No, such comments would have been totally out of character. Although the writer of Hebrews assures us that Jesus knew suffering and temptation just as we do (Heb. 2:18), he didn't grumble. Even on the way to the cross for sins he did not commit, Jesus did not complain.

Over and over the Scriptures tell us to pattern our lives after his. We are to be his representatives (Col. 3:17). That truth means we need to keep working toward that day when we finally will be all Christ saved us for and wants us to be (Phil. 3:12). This process involves checking up on ourselves and asking ourselves some pointed questions: Am I really a Christian? Do I pass the test of putting my faith in Christ alone? Do I feel Christ's presence and power more and more within me (2 Cor. 13:5)? And am I learning to stop complaining?

Compared to the lifestyle of the majority of the world's people, American Christians are richly blessed. Few of us know what it means to be cold, to be hungry, to be homeless, or to own only the clothes on our backs. We live quite comfortably in contrast to the poverty that is the norm in much of the rest of the world. Yet how often we complain—about the weather, the economy, our relatives, our bosses, etc. And how we must hurt the Lord, especially when he hears us complain about the work he has called us to do as Christian writers.

"I didn't even get a letter with the return of my manuscript."

"That editor is impossible. He gets my hopes up by holding my manuscript and then returns it."

"I'm tired of getting only four or five cents a word."

"I'm sick of rejections and long hours in front of my computer. I wonder if it's worth it."

"I doubt anyone reads or appreciates what I write."

On and on our complaints go, especially when we get together with other writers and begin commiserating. People listening to us would never believe we love to write, we believe writing is our ministry, and it is—or should be—a privilege and a joy.

But what are we to do with the very real feelings that trigger our complaints? Are we simply to deny them? Are we being honest with ourselves, God, and others when we force a smile and say only positive things when that's the opposite of how we truly feel?

If anyone had cause to complain about his ministry, it was the apostle Paul. In obedience to the instructions he received on the Damascus Road, he totally committed himself to taking the Gospel of Jesus Christ to the world. He knew this was the work he had been called to. Despite opposition from church leaders, persecution, hardships of every kind, beatings, and even imprisonment, he never wavered.

When he was thrown in the maximum security prison in Philippi (Acts 16:16-40), it would have been understandable for Paul to complain. Reality said his ministry was over. Rarely, if ever, did prisoners leave the inner dungeon alive. His feet were clamped in stocks. His back throbbed with pain from the beating he had unjustly received. If I were Paul, I'm sure I would have said, "I was doing your work, God. How could you allow this to happen to me? It's not fair!"

Yet Acts 16:25 says that Paul and his companion, Silas, prayed and sang hymns to God. Paul lived the advice he later gave to the Philippian Christians: "Always be full of joy in the Lord. . . . Don't worry about anything; instead, pray about everything. . . . Fix your thoughts on what is true and good and right. Think about things that are pure and lovely, and dwell on the fine, good things in others. Think about all you can praise God for and be glad about" (Phil. 4:4, 6, 8).

I believe God is saying, "Stop complaining and toughen up! Rejection slips, low pay, hard work, loneliness, and discouragement go with the territory of being a writer. They are a test of your faith—a test that can make you strong, not in yourself but in me."

As we change our complaints to praises, we discover, like Paul whose chains were broken, that "God can do anything, you know—far more than you could ever imagine or guess or request in your wildest dreams! He does it not by pushing us around but by working within us, his Spirit deeply and gently within us" (Eph. 3:20, *The Message*).

❧

RESPONDING TO GOD'S CALL TO WRITE

Since complaining about our rights and editors is a temptation for most writers, I want to encourage you to turn your thinking around by prayerfully considering "The Editor's Rights" on the next page. Study the listed Scriptures, highlighting those that speak to you of needed change in your life.

THE EDITOR'S RIGHTS

The editor has a right to expect that writers who are Christians will . . .

1. "Follow the Lord's rules" (2 Tim. 2:5).

2. Be honest and keep our word regarding deadlines (Rom. 12:17).

3. Be courteous and wise (James 3:17).

4. Not be critical or give evil reports (James 4:11).

5. Not grumble or complain (James 5:9; Phil. 2:14).

6. Not be bad-tempered or quarrelsome (Eph. 4:31).

7. Evidence the fruit of the Spirit (Gal. 5:22-23).

8. "Work hard and cheerfully" (Col. 3:23; cf. 2 Tim. 2:15).

9. Accept and profit from constructive criticism (Prov. 15:31-32).

10. Be open to new ideas and look for them (Prov. 18:15).

11. Know and responsibly handle God's Word (2 Tim. 2:15).

12. "Leave nothing undone that [we] ought to do" (2 Tim. 4:5).

13. Continually develop our abilities (1 Tim. 4:14-15).

14. Do our very best (Gal. 6:4)

15. Work together as a team (Rom. 12:4-5; Eph. 4:12-13).

21

Winning the Battle

"We don't know what to do, but we are looking to you."
2 CHRONICLES 20:12

Getting into print is like fighting a battle—a battle I was losing! During a writers' conference, three editors requested my book manuscript and then returned it months later, crushing my hopes. The editor of a magazine I contributed to regularly sent back my latest submission with the note, "Sorry, but this wasn't one of your better ones." My mentor, Anne Sirna, tore apart (lovingly) what I thought was one of the best pieces I'd ever written. An assignment wasn't coming together, but then I was too exhausted battling discouragement to have any energy left for writing.

I dumped my frustration on my husband, expecting him to be sympathetic as always. Instead he said, "You know this is part of what it means to be a writer. If you can't handle it, then quit."

"Quit? No!" I exclaimed.

"Then you need to listen to the advice you give others." Paul reached out and hugged me. "Remember how you tell them they need to toughen up and keep praising the Lord?"

I sighed. I knew Paul was right. Like a little child who hadn't gotten her way, I had been pouting instead of praising. Silently I asked the Lord to forgive me and show me how to win the battle.

He reminded me of the prayer chain I organized for the Greater Philadelphia Christian Writers' Fellowship. I encourage our members to use it. Yet even though I felt close to defeat, I had not requested prayer. He also reminded me I had not turned to the Scriptures, something else I encourage them to do.

He led me to the story of King Jehoshaphat in 2 Chronicles 20. Jehoshaphat is in a precarious position. The armies of Moab, Ammon, and the Meunites have declared war on him and the people of Judah. Jehoshaphat is badly shaken by the news that a vast army is marching against him (vv. 2-3). But he doesn't just stand there and wring his hands. He knows his nation needs God's help. He also knows they are not worthy to ask for it. Therefore, he sends out a proclamation that "all the people of Judah should go without food for a time, in penitence and intercession before God" (v. 3).

I can picture people from all over Judah crowding into the temple court. I can hear the hush as Jehoshaphat begins to lead them in prayer. "O Lord God of our fathers—the only God in all the heavens, the Ruler of all the kingdoms of the earth—you are so powerful, so mighty. Who can stand against you?" (v. 6).

Far too often I forget to begin my prayers with praise. I tend to get right to the problem, as if God's time (and mine) is too valuable to waste with preliminaries. But how important these preliminaries are! I must never lose that sense of awe and wonder when I come into the presence of God. He is worthy of my praise, and it is the very act of praising him that changes my perspective and enables me to pray with power.

Jehoshaphat continues his prayer by focusing on all God has done in the past. My memory of God's faithfulness and his ability to use each problem, each trial, for my good is often very short.

"O our God, . . . didn't you give this land forever to the descendants of your friend Abraham?" Jehoshaphat reminds God (v. 7). God has made promises to me too. I've highlighted many of them in my Bible. I don't need to remind God of these promises; I need to remind myself.

"We have no way to protect ourselves against this mighty army," Jehoshaphat admits. "We don't know what to do, but we are looking to you" (v. 12).

When I try to do things in my own strength, God does not intervene. It is only as I surrender the situation to him, as I admit that I am powerless, that I begin to experience his power flowing through me. Like Jehoshaphat, it is then I hear God say, "Don't be afraid or discouraged! . . . For the Lord is with you!" (v. 17).

When King Jehoshaphat heard these words, he fell with his face to the ground and worshipped the Lord. The next morning, in obedience to the Lord, the army of Judah went out to meet the enemy with a choir leading the way. As they began to sing and praise, the Lord caused the enemy to begin fighting amongst themselves. The army of Judah didn't have to strike a single blow!

During the battles that are a part of growing as a writer, how often do I praise the Lord *before* I win the victory? I don't mean just mouthing the words, but falling down before him and worshipping him? Despite circumstances that discourage me and make me feel like giving up, do I recognize his sovereignty and choose to serve him with a thankful heart and "with holy fear and awe" (Heb. 12:28)?

I'd like to tell you I consistently do these things, but I don't. The truth is, the more I come to know the Lord, the more I am aware of the many ways I fall short of what I should be. And yet God, in his mercy and grace, is allowing me to be used in his kingdom work.

In 1992 I taught at the Colorado Christian Writers' Conference, a conference I now direct. I was weary from the spiritual attack I'd been under for weeks, but as I stood to speak, I again experienced God giving me the victory and the empowering of the Holy Spirit. The next day I spent a life-changing time alone with the Lord in the Rocky Mountains. As I drove the steep, winding road to the highest overlook, I felt like I was being drawn into the very presence of God.

"For you are dealing with the one who formed the mountains and made the winds, and knows your every thought," God spoke to me through his Word (Amos 4:13).

Never have I been so aware of his holiness and my unworthiness. Eleven thousand feet above sea level, I knelt and worshipped him. I recommitted myself to the work he has called me to do and asked him to make me strong for the battles yet to come.

I'd known the Lord for well over a quarter of a century, and yet this was the first time I had ever spent such a large block of time alone with him, worshipping him and allowing him to refresh and renew me for the work he is calling me to do. I resolved to make more time to worship him who has already won the battle (2 Chron. 20:15). "Holy, holy, holy, Lord God Almighty—the one who was, and is, and is to come" (Rev. 4:8).

RESPONDING TO GOD'S CALL TO WRITE

When I feel I'm under attack, how often do I, like Jehoshaphat, go to the Lord and seek the support of prayer partners?

How often do I humble myself before the Lord and seek forgiveness for the ways I have failed him?

Am I learning to focus on his greatness, to remember his promises, and to praise him before the battle is won?

How long has it been since I've really taken time to be alone with the Lord simply to worship him? Plan a time now, and put it down on your calendar. Find a place away from the pressures of your home and office, outdoors in the magnificence of God's creation if at all possible.

22

Keeping Fit

You made my body, Lord;
now give me sense to heed your laws.

PSALM 119:73

"Exercise, exercise. Watch me do my exercise." Sometimes I remember the strangest things, like this little ditty we recited in the high school locker room as we exercised the forefinger on both our hands in unison, no less. For most of us, this exercise held much more appeal than calisthenics and running around the track, even though the gym teacher insisted exercise was good for us. We were exercising—our power of coordination and avoidance!

Today, many of my generation still choose to be spectators, rather than participants, in physical activities. Often referred to as couch potatoes, the most exercise we may get in an evening is punching the remote control and going to the kitchen for a snack. Others exercise their fingers on a keyboard or mouse as they spend hours surfing the Internet.

Many are recognizing, however, that our sedentary lifestyles are dangerous to our health and are doing something about it. What about me? I'm trying! For too many years I ignored not just my need for exercise but also healthy eating and sleeping habits. Too much of the wrong foods and too little physical activity have resulted in arthritic knees and excess pounds.

Romans 12:1 (NIV) tells us to offer our bodies "as living sacrifices, holy and pleasing to God—this is your spiritual act of worship." *The Message* says, "God helping you: Take your everyday, ordinary life—your sleeping, eating, going-to-work, and walking-around life—and place it before God as an offering. . . . Readily recognize what he wants from you, and quickly respond to it" (vv. 1-2).

For all who hope to honor and serve God and especially for writers who, by the very nature of our work, sit so much of the time, taking care of the bodies he has given us is critical to our long-term job performance.

Help! This is conviction time—for *me*, especially. But rather than beat myself up for getting so out of shape, I need to affirm, "Today is the first day of the rest of my life." And so, with his help, I'm working to make changes in three areas.

Food. I grew up in a family where food was used both as a reward and punishment. These wrong attitudes carried over into my adult life. Emotions, much more than genuine hunger, tend to dictate what and when I eat.

During a time of high stress a year ago, I frequently wandered into the kitchen, grabbing anything that wasn't nailed down. My photo and even the Scriptures on the frig didn't help. What finally did help was confessing, both to the Lord and my prayer partners, that my eating was out of control. Today I rarely eat between meals. When I do, I know I'm not coping and that I need to ask for an extra measure of God's strength.

There are a lot more changes I need to consistently make in order to glorify the Lord with my eating and bring my weight down to where it needs to be. Some days I do better than others at eating fresh fruits and vegetables and limiting fats and sugars. Preplanning meals, instead of throwing something together at the last minute when I'm starved, helps.

Exercise. If you're like me, you're probably not very good at sticking to a regimen of jumping jacks and sit-ups. I find such exercise totally unappealing even though I know I need to exercise, and not just to keep physically fit. Exercise also sharpens me mentally and helps me to feel good emotionally, yet my exercise bike sits rusting on the back porch, and I can't find my Christian aerobics tape. It's probably in the same place as that book, *It's Here Somewhere*, if I can just remember where I put it!

The Message says, "If you know the right thing to do and don't do it, that, for you, is evil" (James 4:17). And so, again, I need to repent and seek wisdom for what will work for me. Being a person who multi-tasks, I'm more likely to exercise if I can combine it with something else, especially something fun.

Years ago, when my daughter ice skated competitively, I skated with her. Today my husband and I take walks in a nearby park with our golden retriever. My garden needs frequent weeding, and as often as I can I go swimming.

Sleep. I'm a nightowl. I'm also an earlybird. In other words, I'm guilty of burning the candle on both ends. I can get so much done when the phone doesn't ring and there are no interruptions. But what about sleep? If you've ever been to my writers' seminar, you've heard me say, "Sleep is a waste of time."

Dr. Jan W. Kuzma and Cecil Murphey, in an upcoming book tentatively titled *Our Bodies—God's Temple: Living Longer, Healthier, and Happier,* affirm just the opposite: "Getting seven to nine hours of sleep a night is one strong indicator of better health. If we sleep more or get by on less, we literally shorten our life expectancy" (Nashville, TN: Word, 2000).

Obviously, I need to stop depriving my body of rest. I also need to limit the caffeine I drink so that sleeplessness is not an excuse to get up and work. And when the stress of too many deadlines or unsolved problems is the cause of sleeplessness, I need to count blessings, not sheep.

Learning to eat right, exercise, and get enough sleep are important self-disciplines that affect everything else I do, including my writing. They are evidence of my commitment to obey God "with deep reverence, shrinking back from all that might displease him" (Phil. 2:12). I'm so grateful God promises to be "at work within [me], helping [me] want to obey him, and then helping [me] do what he wants" (Phil. 2:13).

Responding to God's Call to Write

This has been a tough chapter to write. Even though God gives me the desire and strength to walk in obedience, bad habits are not easy to break. There are still days I fail and get terribly down on myself. I'm discovering that I need not just to repent but also to learn to love myself as he loves me.

Examine your life, and seek forgiveness for those areas where you struggle to obey him. Then as you read the following poem, ask him to show you how you need to better love yourself.

LOVING ME

No matter what I can do—
how eloquently I express myself,
how great my accomplishments,
how many my talents—
If I do not love others
and myself,
they will count for nothing.
All my knowledge will be empty;
my mountain-moving faith, pointless;
my gifts to the poor, vain.
I must first love myself as God loves me;
then I can love others as myself.
Love is being patient with me
when I am slow learning the lessons
the Lord would teach me.
Love is kind.
It does not allow me
to compare myself to others,
to put myself down,
to punish myself for my mistakes.
Love means believing in the potential
God has placed within me
and trusting him to bring about
my completeness in him.

23

Crisis of Confidence

When I am weak, then I am strong—the less I have,
the more I depend on him.

2 CORINTHIANS 12:10

Suddenly everything seemed to be getting in the way of my writing. Other things, good things, were demanding time and energy. I didn't see how I could say no. When I walked past my office and felt a twinge of guilt, I told myself my hectic schedule was only temporary. Besides, I couldn't let people down when they were depending on me.

One day Anne Sirna, my writing mentor, helped me to see what was happening. "You're running from the very thing you most want to do," she said. "You're running from your writing. Don't you see?" she explained when I looked puzzled. "New writing opportunities are stretching before you and, to put it bluntly, you're scared. You're protecting yourself from the possibility of failure by becoming so involved with other things that you have an excuse not to write."

She's right. I am still afraid of failure, I admitted to myself. *I don't have confidence in my writing ability. And I've been saying yes to other things to avoid having to prove myself.*

"It's a cop-out to see yourself as a failure," she continued, as if reading my thoughts. "You've served your apprenticeship. It's time to move on—to make a commitment to being successful even though success is a lonely and risky thing."

Everyone who is serious about writing will face similar turning points when the choice must be made—move ahead or turn back. Repeatedly, we will be forced to ask ourselves if we are willing to overcome our self-centered fear of failure, if doing God's will is more important to us than the acceptance and approval of men.

It is not just beginning writers who feel anxious when starting a new project or mailing a completed manuscript. We all yearn for acceptance and approval. Even established writers know their work may not be accepted. Success brings with it a heavier responsibility to produce quality work. Self-expectations, as well as the expectations of others, become greater along with the fear that we will not be able to measure up. At any moment a "crisis of confidence," as Anne calls it, can occur.

It can be triggered by many things. We may feel trapped in an interminably long period of writer's block. An editor may require a rewrite of something we felt was our very best work. A manuscript we were sure would be accepted may be returned. It may even be a manuscript we wrote on assignment. I remember when that happened to me. I was devastated! Besides the blow to my ego, I felt I had let the editor down. He expected me to produce something he could use.

I had reached one of those turning points. I could choose to play it safe and turn down future assignments. Or I could accept them (and even seek them) despite my feelings of inadequacy. Or I could give up and quit.

I remember flipping through the pages of my Bible. Colossians 1:29 leaped out: "This is my work, and I can do it only because Christ's mighty energy is at work within me."

Knowing that Paul wrote those words from prison made them even more meaningful to me. I imagined how the Evil One must have used that time to try to persuade Paul to question his call. Surely he did not miss the opportunity to remind Paul of past failures, as well as the times of hardship and hostility. Paul's spirit had absorbed rebuffs and criticism, even from fellow Christians. His body carried the scars of beatings and lashings.

"Is it worth it?" Satan must have whispered more than once. "If

God really called you to be a missionary, then why is he allowing you to rot here in prison?"

But Paul chose to remain true to his call to spread the Good News by writing letters that might otherwise not have been written. "What has happened to me has really served to advance the gospel," he wrote (Phil. 1:12, NIV).

But Paul met the Lord on the Damascus Road, I thought to myself. *He knew Jesus much more intimately than I do.*

Yes, I could argue that Paul had a greater measure of faith because of these experiences. Yet he also knew what it meant to go from tremendous spiritual highs to deep lows and to be plagued with a thorn in his flesh. If, as some commentators suggest, Paul had epilepsy or an eye disease, it must have caused him to wrestle with doubts. How could he preach if he might have a seizure, or write if he could not see?

God did not remove the thorn. Instead, he told Paul, "I am with you; that is all you need. My power shows up best in weak people" (2 Cor. 12:9). Paul chose to rely on this promise and to affirm: "When I am weak, then I am strong—the less I have, the more I depend on him" (2 Cor. 12:10).

The cure for a crisis of confidence is to reexamine in what or, more importantly, in whom, we have placed our confidence. "I know the one in whom I trust," Paul wrote to Timothy (2 Tim. 1:12). That's the key. It's not self-confidence, but God-confidence!

"Stir into flame the strength and boldness that is in you," Paul counseled Timothy (2 Tim. 1:6). Does that mean he expected Timothy never to be afraid? No! "I came to you in weakness—timid and trembling," Paul admitted to the Christians in Corinth (1 Cor. 2:3). And he didn't go to Corinth until his second missionary journey.

"Stand steady, and don't be afraid of suffering for the Lord," Paul encouraged Timothy. "Bring others to Christ. Leave nothing undone that you ought to do" (2 Tim. 4:5). The NIV reads, "discharge all the duties of your ministry."

If a crisis of confidence is holding you back from the work you know you have been called to do, it's time to acknowledge that it's not self-confidence you need but God-confidence. It's time to learn what it means "to be a living demonstration of Christ's power, instead of showing off [your] own power and abilities" (2 Cor. 12:9). And instead of running from opportunities to serve the Lord, you need to continue to focus your life and your ministry on the "firm, tested, precious Cornerstone that is safe to build on. He who believes need never run away again" (Isa. 28:16).

~~~

RESPONDING TO GOD'S CALL TO WRITE

Fear of failure, rejection, writer's block, or not measuring up, can all create a paralyzing crisis of confidence. Read and reflect on the following antidotes to fear, noting beside each reference how God is personally speaking to you.

Psalm 9:10

Psalm 16:8

Psalm 25:3

Psalm 34:4

Isaiah 41:10

Philippians 1:6

1 John 4:18

24

Reaching Our Readers

~≈©

But the wisdom that comes from heaven is first of all
pure and full of quiet gentleness. . . .
It is wholehearted and straightforward and sincere.
JAMES 3:17

Bill Hybels, in a chapter titled "Preaching to Seekers" in
Communicate with Power (edited by Michael Duduit, Grand
Rapids: Baker, 1996, p. 74), says, "Much of what we have to do is
attempt to speak to people's brokenness, their addictions, their
wounds, their victimizations." The same holds true for Christian
writers. We must show our readers how the Gospel is relevant to
these very real needs if God is to use our words to make a difference
in their lives. How can we do this effectively both in writing and
talking to needy people? Here are a number of ways:

   *Avoid pat, simplistic answers to complex and serious prob-
lems.* People who are hurting need more than spiritual Band-Aid™
bandages. We must not demean them and their problems by offering quick fix-its. Instead, we need to give them the gift of encouragement (and one or two realistic steps they can begin to take in
their journeys to wholeness.

   Guard against a critical, judgmental attitude. Paraphrasing
an old Native American proverb, we should not judge anyone
before we have walked a mile in his moccasins. Far too often, we
pass judgment without having been there first. We write from the

top of our heads instead of the depth of our hearts. Always ready to point out the shortcomings in others, we fail to extend the same grace and mercy God extends to us.

Perhaps subconsciously we feel our own sins are minimized when we judge others. Yet Jesus said, "Do not judge, or you too will be judged" (Matt. 7:1, NIV). *The Message* says, "Don't pick on people, jump on their failures, criticize their faults—unless, of course, you want the same treatment."

Harsh, judgmental words not only hurt, they push people away from the Savior rather than draw them to him.

Don't lay guilt trips on your readers. We need to recognize that it is the Holy Spirit's job to convict readers of sin, not ours. When I compiled *My Turn to Care—Affirmations for Caregivers of Aging Parents* (Nashville: Nelson, 1994), I knew that many caregivers were already beating themselves up for not doing more for their aging parents and for not being more patient, loving, kind, etc. They didn't need more guilt trips; they needed encouragement. Blanket statements and such words as "should," "must," and "you" in submissions were immediate red flags that almost always resulted in the return of the manuscript.

Be sensitive to needs and feelings. I remember the time a lay witness mission visited my church. Joyfully and exuberantly, they spoke of God's healing of loved ones in response to their prayers. I wanted to rejoice with them, but my focus was drawn to a dear friend who had recently lost her husband. I winced as I thought of how their well-meaning witness was affecting her and the others. In the hushed silence, I could almost hear their anguish and unspoken questions: Why, Lord? Why didn't you answer my prayers? Didn't I have enough faith? Don't you love me as much as you love these others?

Jesus' promise is not to save us from life's difficulties but to be with us in them and to work good through them (Rom. 8:28, 35–39). Although miraculous answers to prayer are a powerful witness, remember that some readers may still be waiting for answers to their requests. Be sensitive to this fact and consider whether an example of God's sustaining power may offer more encouragement. When we share how God enables us to cope with and rise above the painful realities of life, we are a witness to his awesome keeping power.

Be passionate but guard against being opinionated. There are many differing viewpoints and interpretations of Scripture among

Christians. I have no doubt that when we meet the Lord face to face we're all going to find how much we didn't clearly understand (1 Cor. 13:12). Wise Christians do not present their opinions as the Gospel. We are not God.

Refuse to get drawn into foolish arguments. When our daughter was growing up, we were convinced she was going to be a lawyer. No matter what the subject, she'd always take the opposing view. Now that she's an adult (and about ready to graduate from medical school), she has put away—at least most of the time—her need to assert her independence by arguing with us about everything.

Some people never outgrow the need to pick and win arguments. The apostle Paul counseled Timothy: "Don't get involved in foolish arguments which only upset people and make them angry. God's people must not be quarrelsome; they must be gentle, patient teachers of those who are wrong. Be humble when you are trying to teach those who are mixed up concerning the truth. For if you talk meekly and courteously to them they are more likely, with God's help, to turn away from their wrong ideas and believe what is true" (2 Tim. 2:23-25).

Be careful, and prayerful, to build up rather than tear down. Sadly, we Christians have earned the reputation of "shooting our wounded." At the very time when those who have fallen need grace and mercy, we all too frequently forget Jesus' words: "If any one of you is without sin, let him be the first to throw a stone" (John 8:7, NIV). Gordon MacDonald, a pastor who fell and has been restored and who now preaches the gospel of the "second chance," said in a sermon, "We have come to love the subject of grace because along with repentance it changes lives and refuses to permit Satan the ultimate victory."

Don't compromise the truth, but also don't force it on others. "Let your conversation be gracious as well as sensible," Paul says in Colossians 4:6. Peter says that if anybody asks us why we believe as we do, we need to "be ready to tell him, and do it in a gentle and respectful way" (1 Pet. 3:15).

Often we Christians are viewed as attacking anyone and anything we do not agree with rather than calmly and clearly, graciously and sensibly, presenting biblical truth. We need to be respectful (1 Tim. 5:1), speak the truth in love (Eph. 4:15), and be winsome rather than obnoxious.

Always remember the need for love and compassion. God loved the world so much that he sent his Son, not "to condemn the world, but to save the world through him" (John 3:17, NIV). Jesus had compassion on the weary and heavy-laden, the sick and the poor, the outcast, and the sinner. We can do no less if we hope to show them how God has called us, and is calling them, out of the darkness into his wonderful light (1 Pet. 2:9).

RESPONDING TO GOD'S CALL TO WRITE

Read Paul's sermon on Mars Hill in Acts 17:16-34. List below the needs he perceived his listeners had and how he addressed and sought to meet them.

25

Like Peter

~~

You have been chosen by God himself—
you are priests of the King.

1 PETER 2:9

I've often written about the apostle Paul. If there was an early Christian workaholic, it was Paul. Undaunted by opposition and persecution, he traveled throughout the Roman world spreading the Gospel. Even when he settled in one place, he filled every hour with preaching, teaching, and tent making. His mind and hands were never idle!

I admire Paul, but I love Peter. In a special, winsome way I see his feelings and failings in the pages of the New Testament; and I feel close to him.

The first time Peter's words are recorded in the gospel of Luke (5:1-11), he makes himself transparent. He was washing his nets beside the seashore while Jesus preached nearby. Noticing the empty boats, Jesus stepped into one and asked Peter to push it out into the water. I can picture Peter forgetting the nets and listening to Jesus. When Jesus finished speaking, he instructed Peter to go into deeper water and let down the nets.

Logic told Peter this action was foolish. They had worked hard all night and caught nothing. Daytime fishing was a waste of time, but he obeyed Jesus. And what incredible results! The nets were so full they began to tear. Peter didn't stop to analyze what had happened or to see who might be watching. He fell down on his knees and said, "Oh, sir, please leave us—I'm too much of a sinner for you to have around" (v. 8). When they got to shore, he left everything and followed Jesus.

From then on, Peter stayed close to Jesus. He was always up front, directing the crowds and speaking for the other disciples. Was Peter simply a naturally gifted leader? I'm not so sure. I can't help but wonder if Peter was trying to prove himself. He may have thought the others (even those who were also fishermen) were more likely candidates for discipleship. John was a deep thinker. Andrew was outgoing. James had studied the law.

The more Peter tried, the more he failed. He walked on water, only to sink (Matt. 14:22-32). He was the first of the Twelve to boldly confess, "You are the Messiah," only to be rebuked a short time later for trying to tell Jesus what to do (Mark 8:27-33). He boasted of his loyalty to the Master, only to deny him (John 13:36-38). Yet on the day of Pentecost, Peter was transformed from a coward into a Spirit-filled preacher and leader (Acts 2:14-41). Even before the mighty Sanhedrin, he stood his ground. "We cannot stop telling about the wonderful things we saw Jesus do and heard him say" (Acts 4:20).

What can Christian writers learn from Peter? I believe he shows us what must happen in our lives when we come face to face with Jesus Christ. Like Peter, we need to confess our sins, recognizing that Jesus "personally carried the load of our sins in his own body when he died on the cross, so that we can be finished with sin and live a good life from now on" (1 Pet. 2:24). If our words are to have credibility, our walk needs to match our talk.

Peter also shows us the importance of obedience, of being willing to leave what we are doing to follow Jesus into unknown situations. The safe thing to do would have been for Peter to stay on the fringes of Jesus' life and ministry. He could have continued with his fishing business and taken time off only when Jesus was in town. But Peter chose to risk everything and follow Jesus.

I'm not suggesting anyone quit his job and go into a full-time writing ministry. I don't know many who are called to make a living at writing. But we can ask the Lord to help us give up some things we enjoy doing in order to make time for writing. Those who are called to write from personal experience can ask for strength to write openly of the lessons God has taught them in order to minister to the needs of their readers.

"Feed my sheep," Jesus told Peter after his resurrection (John 21:17, NIV). No doubt Peter was still reeling from his denial of Jesus. Three times Jesus gave Peter the opportunity to reaffirm his commitment, and three times he challenged Peter to feed his sheep. Again Peter obeyed. He learned to care for the flock "willingly, not grudgingly; not for what [he] would get out of it but because [he was] eager to serve the Lord" (1 Pet. 5:2).

We need to be ready to share our faith "and do it in a gentle and respectful way" (1 Pet. 3:15). "Preach [write] as though God himself were speaking through you," Peter says (1 Pet. 4:11). "Be ready to suffer" (1 Pet. 4:1) but focus on the "wonderful joy ahead, even though the going is rough for a while down here" (1 Pet. 1:6).

Another lesson from Peter is how to deal with our egos. We are to "serve each other with humble spirits" (1 Pet. 5:5). Like Peter, we must be willing to give "all honor to God, the God and Father of our Lord Jesus Christ; for it is his boundless mercy that has given us the privilege of being born again" (1 Pet. 1:3). We must desire to point others to Jesus, not to ourselves.

Peter provides a lot more practical help that has direct application to our lives as writers. "Be clear minded and self-controlled so that you can pray" (1 Pet. 4:7, NIV). "Keep on doing what is right and trust yourself to the God who made you, for he will never fail you" (1 Pet. 4:19). "Stand firmly in his love" (1 Pet. 5:12).

In 2 Peter 1:2-8, he describes ways to "grow strong spiritually and become fruitful and useful to our Lord Jesus Christ." Why? It's a process! It was for him and will be for us. Like Peter, there will be times when we will fail. But he rose above his failures, and we can too.

At Bill Gothard's Institute in Basic Youth Conflicts, I received a button with the letters *PBPGINFWMY.* They stand for the sentence, "Please be patient; God is not finished with me yet." We also need to be patient with ourselves. Our faith is going to be tested (1 Pet. 1:7). Sometimes it may be found wanting. But the amount of our faith (remember what Jesus said in Luke 17:6 about faith the size of a mustard seed?) is not as important as the One we believe in. Truly, he will "never disappoint those who trust in him" (1 Pet. 2:6). He has chosen us and will equip us so that, through the words we write and the lives we live, we will effectively be able to "show to others how God called [us] out of the darkness into his wonderful light" (1 Pet. 2:9).

RESPONDING TO GOD'S CALL TO WRITE

Read 1 and 2 Peter. Note below those passages that specifically speak to you and your call to feed the flock of God through your writing. Commit one verse to memory today, and ask God to work it into the fabric of your life.

26

Conquering the Deadly Ds

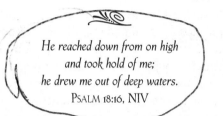

He reached down from on high
and took hold of me;
he drew me out of deep waters.
PSALM 18:16, NIV

Computer viruses are scary! "Do *not* open this file; or *everything* on your hard drive will be destroyed, and your drive will be corrupted. This is not a hoax but a deadly virus."

I don't know if these messages are hoaxes or not. I've been told it's unwise to pass them along since a virus can be attached to the message. I quickly delete them and pray my virus protection software is doing its job. So far, thank the Lord, my computer is free of deadly viruses.

But what of the deadly viruses that attack my mind and heart? As a Christian who seeks to write his answer, I find I'm especially prone to the virus known as the Deadly Ds.

What are the Deadly Ds? Could you already be infected?

Probably. I don't know any writers who have a natural immunity to the Deadly Ds of disappointment, discouragement, doubt, and despair.

It all starts when I'm exposed to disappointment. I may bring it on myself by unrealistic expectations. Although I'm certainly not a mathematical genius, even I can comprehend that my odds of acceptance are slim when the *Christian Writers' Market Guide* says a periodical is only one percent freelance written or they accept only one or two articles a year. That's why, in the seminar I teach, I emphasize the importance of learning which markets offer the best opportunities for publication. But even submitting to a market that is one hundred percent freelance written doesn't guarantee acceptance.

Someone has said you're not a professional writer until you've received one thousand rejection slips. One thousand! That's a lot of disappointments, especially if, like me, you've struggled all your life with feeling rejected.

Harry Edward Neal, the author of over thirty books, says, "View rejection slips as scout badges, evidence of perseverance and determination." Since I've received three to four thousand [I've stopped counting!], my scout sash is getting mighty heavy. I thank God I've also had over a thousand sales, so my rejection/acceptance ratio isn't bad. I've learned to call them returns, but they still hurt.

"Why, God? Why aren't you opening the doors?" It's a legitimate question; but if we listen closely, we may find the tone of our voice bordering on a whine. Diagnosis? Disappointments have made us vulnerable to discouragement. Left unchecked, doubts will get a stranglehold on us next. Then despair will follow as the Deadly Ds disable us. I know. I've been there.

In chapter 13, "Disappointed but Not Discouraged," we looked at how Jesus handled disappointments. And in chapter 23, "Crisis of Confidence," we learned from the apostle Paul that God-confidence is more important than self-confidence. But there's still more I believe God wants me to say about the third Deadly D, self-doubt.

Although many people in the Bible struggled with self-doubts, I think especially of the prophet Jeremiah. His ministry spanned forty-one years and five kings, but it almost never got off the ground. Known as the reluctant prophet, when God's call came to Jeremiah, he said, "I can't do that! I'm far too young! I'm only a youth!" (Jer. 1:6). Some of us may say, "I'm far too old!" Or "I'm not creative enough!" Or, and this has been the biggie in my life, "I don't have enough education!"

For years I battled, not very successfully, a crushing sense of inferiority because I am not a college graduate. Truth is, I've not had even one day of college. That used to make me feel terribly ashamed. How presumptuous to think a high school graduate could write for the Lord, much less teach others to write! But then one day someone asked me, "Do you believe God is omnipotent and omniscient?"

"Yes, he is all powerful and all knowing," I replied. (I have a hard a time pronouncing the words she used.)

"And do you believe God has a perfect plan for your life?"

"Yes," I replied again.

"Then if God, in his omnipotence and omniscience, chose for you not to have a college education, why are you grieving him by coveting what he chose not to give you?"

Never have I been so immediately convicted of sin. Right there in the restaurant, I bowed my head and sought his forgiveness.

A year later, God gave me the opportunity to keynote at a writers' conference in New York. As I shared this story with my hostess, Jan Wise, it was obvious to her that I still struggled with a sense of lack. We began to pray, but suddenly she stopped. "God has just shown me—you've been homeschooled by the Father. And only special kids are homeschooled!"

Education, or lack thereof, may not be an issue for you. But more than likely, there's something else that feeds your self-doubts. It may be voices from your childhood, the cutting words of a close friend, or perhaps even the put-downs of your spouse. One thing is certain, the Evil One knows where you're most vulnerable. The more he sees you as a threat, the more fiercely he will attack.

Can we recover from the Deadly Ds? Of course, as long as we submit ourselves to the care of the Great Physician. But we must remember that the virus will always be latent. We need to faithfully follow the Doctor's orders: "Be careful—watch out for attacks from Satan, your great enemy. He prowls around like a hungry, roaring lion, looking for some victim to tear apart. Stand firm when he attacks. Trust the Lord; and remember that other Christians all around the world [and other Christian writers] are going through these sufferings too. . . . God, who is full of kindness through Christ . . . personally will come and pick you up, and set you firmly in place, and make you stronger than ever" (1 Pet. 5:8-10).

RESPONDING TO GOD'S CALL TO WRITE

"Do you want to get well?" Jesus asked the man who had been an invalid for thirty-eight years (John 5:6, NIV). "It was not so foolish a question as it may sound," William Barclay says. "The man had waited for thirty-eight years and it might well have been that hope had died and left behind a passive and dull despair" (*The Gospel of John*, vol. 1, Louisville, KY: Westminster John Knox, 1975, p. 179).

When we've got a bad case of the Deadly Ds, we may not have the strength or energy to get well. It may be easier just to give in, especially if we're not certain God is calling us to write. (See chapter 4.) But Barclay also says, "When we have intensity of desire and determination to make the effort, hopeless though it may seem, the power of Christ gets its opportunity, and with him we can conquer what for long has conquered us" (p. 180).

To get started on the road to recovery, or prevent a relapse, do a topical Bible study of the following subjects:

Success vs. disappointment

Courage vs. discouragement

Faith vs. doubt

Hope vs. despair

27

Finish What You Start

> *I want to suggest that you finish
> what you started to do.*
> 2 CORINTHIANS 8:10

I knew God had called me to write a book. I worked for weeks gathering notes. Using *Books in Print* and catalogs from Christian publishing houses, I did my market research. Almost nothing was available on my topic. I sensed I was ahead of the market; but since the secular press was addressing the issue, I hoped Christian publishers would not be far behind.

The more I worked, the more enthusiastic I became. I saw how my book would meet a real need. I felt the Lord's guidance as the chapter-by-chapter synopsis fell into place. I committed myself and my book to the Lord and asked him to help me write it to his glory.

I'd like to say that from that point on everything went smoothly—that I faithfully sat down to write each day, completed my book in record time, found a publisher immediately, and saw it make the best-seller list. The truth is I got bogged down and discouraged. My enthusiasm and commitment waned. It became easier and easier to procrastinate.

Although I knew God wanted the book written, I doubted my ability to write it. I felt overwhelmed and inadequate. I was afraid to take the risk of pouring myself into a book—especially a book that meant dealing with painful memories.

"And what makes you think you can find a publisher if you get it finished?" the Evil One taunted me.

A workshop Lee Roddy taught at a 1980 Christian writers' conference, a workshop I had *not* intended to take, was the turning point. Lee said to the class, "God chose you. As you abide in him, your life will bring forth fruit." On the closing day, he prayed that "heaven would be different" because of what we would write. He challenged us, if we felt moved by God, to make a commitment to complete our book within a year. I knew God was speaking to me. With a pounding heart and shaking hand I put my commitment in writing.

During the next year, I found that making a commitment and keeping it are two different things. Daily I made excuses to work on everything but the book. Ideas that had sat in file folders for years now begged to be written. But when I wrote and submitted these short pieces, they all started coming back. Lee refused to feel sorry for me. "You must ask and seek God's reason. I can offer a suggestion: It's time for you to move on."

A friend remarked that a thousand years in God's sight are like a day (Ps. 90:4). But I knew God knew my commitment was to complete the book in a 365-day year. Yet now, with only three months to go, how would I ever finish in time?

One spring day, I sat down beside a stream in a state park. "God, please speak to me," I prayed. The wind blew the pages of my Bible to 2 Corinthians 8:10-11: "I want to suggest that you finish what you started to do. . . . Let your enthusiastic idea at the start be equalled by your realistic action now."

And so, finally, I got to work. Some days all I had to give God was my willingness. But it was enough! With his help, I completed the book—exactly to the day! I mailed it to a publisher I had previously queried. For five months I counted the days and prayed. The more time passed, the more I felt certain it was going to be accepted. But one day, the mailman handed me a package. My heart sank. It was my manuscript with a "Sorry this doesn't meet our needs" note.

The process began all over again. Over a six-year period, I queried forty-one publishers! Often I didn't get to first base. Other times, I was asked to send the manuscript only to have it returned—

again. But God kept encouraging me to send it out again, and he kept giving me promises to sustain me.

"And let us not get tired of doing what is right, for after a while we will reap a harvest of blessing if we don't get discouraged and give up," I read in Galatians 6:9. I circled and dated it. The very next day the manuscript came back. It had reached the final stages of the review process where they told me they accepted one in three manuscripts. But my manuscript wasn't the one! I don't think I would have been able to start all over again with the query process (and do yet another rewrite) if it had not been for the promise in Galatians and other Scriptures.

I vividly remember the night a well-meaning friend said, "It seems to me that if God wanted your book published, it would be in print by now." Somehow I managed to bite my tongue and not let her know how angry her words made me. How dare she or anyone assume that if God is in something, he will bless it by making the process quick and easy. We forget that he did not even spare his own Son from taking the difficult and painful road to the cross.

Another friend suggested I had written the book for practice. I felt like throwing the manuscript at her. Instead, I gritted my teeth and plodded on.

More out of habit than hope, I talked to editors at writers' conferences. I had my sales pitch memorized. Many asked me to send the entire manuscript. My postage bill was getting astronomical—and so was my discouragement—as the manuscript kept coming back.

Finally, my "Please, Lord, let the book be accepted" prayers began to change. "It's your manuscript, Lord. Let your will, not mine, be done." Each time I prayed that prayer, the pain of rejection diminished. The conviction grew that God was in control.

I heard about a new publishing house and planned to query them. Then, to my surprise, the editor attended my home conference. I made an appointment to talk to him, and he took the manuscript with him. Several months later, he called and asked me to meet with him to talk about the manuscript. "And we'll sign the contract too," he said. I was speechless.

When I received the page proofs, terror gripped me. Did I really want to make myself that vulnerable? I considered calling my editor and saying, "Let's forget this." Yet if even one person could be helped . . .

My first television interview was equally terrifying. "Why did you write this book?" Jim McClellan asked me. My mind went blank! Praise God, what seemed like an eternity must have been only seconds, and I must have answered intelligently because he invited me to return.

Then I knew why it took six years and three months to find a publisher. Back in the beginning, I thought I was ready for the media interviews and speaking that go with writing a book on a sensitive issue. Now I wasn't at all sure I was ready. But that's growth!

"There is a right time for everything" (Eccl. 3:1). "We will reap a harvest of blessing if we don't get discouraged and give up" (Gal. 6:9).

RESPONDING TO GOD'S CALL TO WRITE

Is there something you've started that you need to finish? To help you keep on keeping on, read the following passages about the struggles the apostle Paul endured. Record what you feel God is saying to you.

Galatians 1:13—2:1

2 Corinthians 4:8-18

2 Corinthians 6:3-10

2 Corinthians 11:23-33

28

Burnout

Let be and be still,
and know—recognize and understand—
that I am God.

PSALM 46:10, AMP

"God, I can't! I just can't do it anymore! I'm so tired! I just can't keep on keeping on!"

Whoa! What happened? Notice I did not say "won't"; rather, I said "can't." Why? Because I was burned out! I had pushed so hard for so long that there simply wasn't anything left to give. I was drained, empty.

Webster's New World Dictionary's definition of burnout reads, "To exhaust yourself by too much work." Having gone through several periods of burnout, my definition is much stronger. For me, it is a state of being totally depleted—physically, mentally, emotionally, and spiritually. It is frightening and frustrating since I have used the argument that Christians need not be victims of burnout because of the power of prayer and availability of God's help.

Definitions and arguments aside, it is possible that each of us, no matter how deep our faith, will experience burnout at some point in our lives. It is not a state peculiar to writers; rather, it is the product of the pressure and stress of daily living—the accumulation of problems and never-ending to-do lists that cause us to push ourselves beyond our resources.

"There is a difference between *burning out* for God and *being poured out* for God," Elizabeth Skoglund says. "Burning out will not multiply our results. . . . Burnout will hurt the quality of our work and eventually diminish its quantity as physical or emotional breakdown take hold" (*Burning Out for God,* Downers Grove, IL: InterVarsity, 1988, pp. 15, 18).

The Bible says that God created the world in six days; and on the seventh day, he rested. Surely he has given us an example to follow, yet I know I'm not the only person to ignore it. And I'm not talking about just keeping the Sabbath, as important as I believe that is. We also need to pace ourselves during the week. While an occasional late night in the office can produce wonderful results, it's not the ultimate answer.

"Rest in the Lord; wait patiently for him to act," David said (Ps. 37:7). I've always found it difficult to live by that verse. It's not just my problem with impatience but the problem I have with resting. What does it *really* mean to rest in the Lord?

I used to think it meant a cessation from activity. Ugh! Since I enjoy what I'm doing, I don't find that very appealing. I have a strong sense of call and am excited about the ministry opportunities God has given me. The rest God is talking about, however, is not a sit-and-do-nothing rest but rather, I believe, a state of being so centered in him that we neither run out ahead of him or lag behind. It's learning what it means to abide in him as Jesus spoke of in John 15 and to wait for his clear leading *before* we say yes.

"Come to me and I will give you rest—all of you who work so hard beneath a heavy yoke," Jesus said (Matt. 11:28). Eugene Peterson's paraphrase of Matthew 11:28-30 in *The Message* reads, "Are you tired? Worn out? Burned out on religion? Come to me. Get away with me and you'll recover your life. I'll show you how to take a real rest. Walk with me and work with me—watch how I do it. Learn the unforced rhythms of grace. I won't lay anything heavy or ill-fitting on you. Keep company with me and you'll learn to live freely and lightly."

In 1835, in his beloved hymn, "What a Friend We Have in Jesus," Joseph M. Scriven wrote, "O what peace we often forfeit,/O what needless pain we bear,/All because we do not carry/Everything to God in prayer."

But what about those times when I have prayed and waited on him, those times when I know I'm in the center of his will, yet still I teeter on the edge of burnout? Frequently, the problem is not with the work itself but rather with my attitude. Pushing myself to work long hours because I'm afraid I won't meet a deadline, afraid I won't measure up, robs me of joy and is often counterproductive. I can't do my best work when I'm pushing or rushed. Haste does make waste. And I'm reminded of Jesus' example. Despite only three short years to complete his earthly ministry, he never was rushed or uptight.

Expecting more of myself than is realistic—more than God may expect—contributes to that feeling that my life is out of control and ultimately to burnout. The more overwhelmed I feel, the harder I try to regain control. Instead of stopping to pray and ask the Lord for his perspective of what's most important, I jump from one thing to the next, trying to somehow keep my head above water. But like Peter, taking my eyes off the Lord only causes me to sink (Matt. 14:22-32).

The exhaustion that comes from having given all to reach a goal and the low that naturally follows a high may trigger burnout. I'm reminded of the story of Elijah. After winning an incredible victory over the prophets of Baal, he went from the mountaintop to the valley—actually the pit—of self-pity and depression. "'I've had enough,' he told the Lord" (1 Kings 19:4).

Like Elijah, I, too, have won some victories. I have known the joy of seeing the Lord do "exceeding abundantly above all that [I] ask or think" (Eph. 3:20, KJV). But then I lower my shield of faith because my arms are too weary to hold it up. Immediately, the Evil One takes aim, knowing I'm especially vulnerable to his lies and half-truths when I'm exhausted.

Someone has said the difference between despair and hope is a good night's sleep. The first thing Elijah did was sleep. After he rested, an angel woke him and told him to get up and eat.

Resting and eating sensibly helps me regain my perspective. I see how I have been pushing too hard. Yes, I'm doing kingdom work; but I need to remind myself that the world does not rest on my shoulders. When I complete a major project, I need to stop and rest—and celebrate—rather than immediately tackle the overwhelming piles of catch-up work.

Sometimes, however, burnout is not the result of my attitude or overwork. Problems I haven't created and cannot resolve may be dumped in my lap. After all, I've always been the fix-it person in my family. A loved one may be in a crisis and need my help. Maybe all I can do is listen or stand beside her bed in the emergency room. Or I may offer godly counsel only to find myself in the middle of a situation for which there are no easy answers. Yet whether I'm able to help or not, I've got to try. I can't ignore the needs of those around me; but if I'm not careful and prayerful, I can take on cares and responsibilities that are not mine to carry. I need to remember that I'm called to point people to the Savior, not to try to be their savior.

What of my own needs? I thank God that when I come to him, exhausted and stressed for whatever reason, he doesn't ignore me. He quiets my heart and speaks as he did to Elijah, in a gentle whisper. "Let be and be still" (Ps. 46:10, AMP). He reminds me of his promises and provision for all of my needs. And I know, because he has done it for me again and again, that "he gives power to the tired and worn out, and strength to the weak. They that wait upon the Lord shall renew their strength" (Isa. 40:29, 31).

～◎

RESPONDING TO GOD'S CALL TO WRITE

Read Matthew 11:28-30 in several translations or paraphrases. Then evaluate your present situation. Are you in over your head because you've tried to pick up every loose end and need? If so, seek his forgiveness and ask him to set you free to do what he is calling you to do—no more and no less!

29

Finding Our Place

~~~

We are all parts of it [Christ's body],
and it takes every one of us to make it complete.

ROMANS 12:5

Frequently I receive letters from writers who are questioning their call because they've fallen into the trap of comparing themselves with other writers. Convincing themselves that they don't have what it takes, they are in danger of missing the uniqueness of the gifts God has given them.

It is not the Lord's intention that we be carbon copies of one another. "Christ has given each of us special abilities—whatever he wants us to have out of his rich storehouse of gifts" (Eph. 4:7).

Some, but not all, have the imagination to write fiction. Some are poets. Some have the ability to do the necessary research for well-documented magazine articles. Others are especially gifted to write for children. And still others are evangelists, prophets, and teachers, etc.

"Why is it that he gives us these special abilities to do certain things best? It is that God's people will be equipped to do better work for him, building up the Church, the body of Christ, to a position of strength and maturity" (Eph. 4:12).

As always the Evil One seeks to conquer and divide. It's an old military strategy and one he often uses quite effectively in the writing community. Instead of focusing on the One we are called to serve, we can easily get caught up in the media hype and be wowed by big names and big sales. I'm not saying there's anything wrong in being a best-selling author. What is wrong is the jealousy and competitiveness that comes from coveting fame and fortune. These attitudes can also result in our compromising the message God has given us.

In *Raise Up a Standard—A Challenge to Christian Writers,* Michael Phillips asks, "Do we want to write the *sensational* or the *significant?*" He challenges Christian writers "to be on the cutting edge, not of trends, not of what's going on in publishing, in music, in video, in entertainment, in Hollywood, in Nashville, or in CBA . . . but to be on the cutting edge of what's going on in God's heart. . . . If you believe in your message, don't give up on it. Don't water it down. Don't sensationalize it just to get it published or to try to make it a best-seller. Stand firm, in integrity and truthfulness, for what God has given you to communicate" (Eureka, CA: Sunrise Books, pp. 29-31).

That admonition brings us back to where I started—finding our special place in the body of Christ and the world of Christian publishing. The apostle Paul devoted a good portion of his first letter to the Corinthians comparing Christ's body to our physical bodies. The hands, ears, and eyes are all essential. "The eye can never say to the hand, 'I don't need you.' The head can't say to the feet, 'I don't need you'" (1 Cor. 12:21).

So, too, the effectiveness of Christian literature depends on the diverse skills of many different kinds of writers as well as the expertise of editors, artists, graphic designers, printers, distributors, bookstore managers, publicists, etc. "We each have different work to do," Paul says. "So we belong to each other, and each needs all the others" (Rom. 12:5).

Although we are not all novelists, poets, or devotional writers, and few of us will ever write a best-seller, we do have the responsibility to use our own special gift to its fullest potential.

Someday we are going to meet Christ face to face, and he is going to ask us what we have done with our gift. It is my prayer that I'll be able to show him that I have used it—that I have not allowed my tendency to compare myself with others (and find myself wanting) to limit what he wanted to do through me. I want "the words of my mouth [and my pen] and the meditation of my heart [to] be pleasing in [his] sight" (Ps. 19:14, NIV).

One of the best ways I can grow as a writer and fulfill the role God has given me in the world of Christian publishing is by developing close friendships with other Christian writers. I praise God for the writers' conference at Biola University years ago, where walking back to the dorm one afternoon, I made a forever friend. The Colorado Christian Writers' Conference that Debbie Barker directed for eight years and I now direct, is a result of that "divine encounter."

I also remember the day a young woman, new in the area, called me. Through a series of God incidents, she had found out about me and the Greater Philadelphia Christian Writers' Fellowship that I founded and direct. Again God was at work forming another forever friendship that has changed my life. (See Sue Cameron's poem, "Words," on page 58.)

The night before Jesus went to the cross, he prayed for "future believers"—for you and for me—that we "will be of one heart and mind" (John 17:21). He expects us to love each other, "working together with one heart and mind and purpose" (Phil. 2:2). May each of us know the joy of being encouraged, affirmed, and held accountable by others who are also called to write his answer.

RESPONDING TO GOD'S CALL TO WRITE

If you don't live in an area where there is a Christian writers' conference, consider planning your vacation around a conference that's somewhere you always wanted to visit. Sally Stuart's *Christian Writers' Market Guide* has a listing of national conferences and workshops, as well as groups that meet, plus some Canadian and foreign listings.

If you are not part of a small group that meets regularly for fellowship and critiquing, then find or form one. See Appendix 6 for how-tos. If you already belong to a group, you may want to use this book as a study resource as other groups have done. May God bring you into rich fellowship with other Christians who write.

TEACH ME, O LORD, THY HOLY WAY
by William T. Matson, 1833-1906

Teach me, O Lord, Thy holy way,
And give me an obedient mind,
That in Thy service I may find
My soul's delight from day to day.

Guide me, O Savior, with Thy hand,
And so control my thoughts and deeds
That I may tread the path which leads
Right onward to the blessed land.

Help me, O Savior, here to trace
The sacred footsteps Thou hast trod,
And, meekly walking with my God,
To grow in goodness, truth, and grace.

Bless me in every task, O Lord,
Begun, continued done for Thee;
Fulfill Thy perfect work in me;
And Thine abounding grace afford.

30

Prepare the Way

~≈©

*Make the most of your chances
to tell others the Good News.*
Colossians 4:5

Will this be the year, month, week, or even the day when Jesus returns? He tells us to "stay awake and be prepared" (Matt. 25:13). Doing so involves more than just sitting and observing the signs of the times. As Christian writers, we have the privilege and responsibility to wait actively, pointing to those signs and presenting Christ's life alternative to our hurting world. We share with John the Baptist the task of preparing the way for Christ's coming.

This work of preparation needs to begin on a personal level. Like John, we need to be doing specific things in order to become the best possible communicators of God's truth. John didn't just stumble into his ministry as a forerunner. He prepared himself. He lived alone in the wilderness. He wore clothes woven from camel hair and a leather belt and ate locusts and wild honey (Mark 1:4, 6).

I'm not suggesting we leave our homes and families and move to some desolate spot. Nor am I suggesting we throw out our wardrobes and go on a fad diet. I know I couldn't eat a locust! But we do need to give some prayerful thought to John's example of preparation.

John gave top priority to spending time with God and listening to his voice. He knew it was essential that he keep a servant's heart and not lose sight of his call to point to the Christ. "He must become greater; I must become less," he said (John 3:30, NIV). How much time have we committed to being with the Lord, listening to him, and making certain our actions are in line with his will for our lives?

John lived a very simple lifestyle. What steps are we taking to free ourselves from the clutter of things and activities in order to respond to God's call to write?

John ate natural foods. He took care of his health. Do we regularly examine our eating habits and make needed changes? Have we gotten lazy about exercise? (See chapter 22.) Remember, our bodies are the temples of God's Holy Spirit. He expects us to take care of them.

What was John's message? Isaiah foretold that he would be "a voice shouting from the barren wilderness, 'Prepare a road for the Lord to travel on! Widen the pathway before him!'" (Luke 3:4).

Having prepared ourselves daily for the ministry of writing, we need, in faith, to see that ministry widening and expanding. It's time to take the limits off God! If you know he has given you a message that needs to be written, then write it. If you've had some work published but lately you've gotten lazy, you need to recommit yourself to your writing ministry. Prayerfully set some measurable goals and get to work.

If you're a beginner and are reluctant to submit that first manuscript, then get up the courage to read it to a critique group. Make the necessary revisions, take a leap of faith, and mail it. It will never touch anyone in your desk drawer. If you know you need to learn more, join a workshop, go to a conference, take a creative writing class, or enroll in a correspondence course. But do something! Make room in your heart and life for the work God is calling you to do. Widen that pathway!

"Level the mountains! Fill up the valleys! Straighten the curves! Smooth out the ruts!" (Luke 3:5). This verse speaks to me about the need for maturity.

Our work as writers cannot be ruled by the ups and downs of our feelings. Beyond every mountain is another valley. Some days our writing efforts will seem futile. Like the early settlers who walked beside their wagons all the way to the west coast, we may wonder if we'll ever get there. But God encourages us to "stand firm" on legs that are often shaky and "mark out a straight, smooth path" for our feet (Heb. 12:12-13).

He calls us to follow him over the mountains and through the valleys—to stay on that narrow road that leads to life (Matt. 7:14). He challenges us to walk in obedience and watch out for the ruts along the way that can so easily cause us to stumble. The ruts are different for each one of us. For me, they are the bad habits I keep falling into that limit my effectiveness and cause me to become discouraged. I need to look before I step. With his help, I can walk around that negative thought, the telephone, procrastination, etc.

It takes hard work to conquer bad habits, walk in obedience, prepare the way for Christ's return. Weariness, frustration, and discouragement can become troublesome traveling companions. They certainly must have been for John. Repeatedly, he was grilled by representatives of the "top pops" in Jerusalem. They wanted to know if he was the Messiah, Elijah, or the Prophet. When he answered no, they wanted to know what right he had to baptize (John 1:19-27). But John boldly continued preaching.

John's call to repentance infuriated those who thought they were righteous. Eventually John's honesty and unwillingness to compromise his message led to his arrest. But even in prison, chains could not bind John's spirit. He had a vision! He knew that one day "all mankind shall see the Savior sent from God" (Luke 3:6).

As the day of Christ's return draws ever nearer, let us "remember why he is waiting. He is giving us time to get his message of salvation out to others" (2 Pet. 3:15). Many are facing problems that seem like mountains. Their valleys are so deep they may turn to alcohol or drugs. Others, including teenagers, may try to take their lives. Some will succeed. But we can write words that will point them to the One who can heal their hurts and enable them to cope with life.

He is coming! When he comes I want to be doing the work he has called me to do, making the most of every opportunity to share the Good News (Col. 4:5).

I encourage you to catch a vision for the work he is calling you to do. Commit yourself to it and to him and trust in his promises.

Today is the day to begin preparing the way! Trust him to "make the darkness bright before [you] and smooth and straighten out the road ahead" (Isa. 42:16).

RESPONDING TO GOD'S CALL TO WRITE

In the words of Dennis Rainey, National Director of Family Ministry, Campus Crusade for Christ, "Do you believe that God can give you a vision for your world that will capture you for the rest of your life? . . . What are you uniquely burdened for? What injustice causes you to pound the table and weep?" ("My Soapbox" letter, February 10, 1986). Write your responses below.

Do you really believe God can use you to address these issues? Why or why not?

Ask yourself, "When Jesus returns, what manuscript do I most want to lay at his feet?" Get to work claiming his promise. "Now you have every grace and blessing; very spiritual gift and power for doing his will are yours during this time of waiting for the return of our Lord Jesus Christ" (1 Cor. 1:7).

31

Driven or Led?

❧

*Be careful to do what the Lord your God
has commanded you;
do not turn aside to the right or to the left.*
DEUTERONOMY 5:32, NIV

The wonderful world of pretend. As a youngster growing up in a
not-so-happy family, I visited it frequently. I'd compete against
myself in the "Olympic" event of batting a beach ball in the air,
determined to beat my previous record and improve my "form." A
two-by-four became my "high wire" circus act with Mom's clothes
pole my balancing pole. My bicycle made it possible for me to
escape to the forest preserve half a mile from home. There I spent
many hours in my make-believe world. There my father did not
slap me across my face and lock me in my room.

When I married and moved away from home, I no longer
needed my pretend world. I did, however, desperately need to prove
to my family and myself that I was somebody. Abraham Maslow, in
his hierarchy of needs, refers to this need as self-actualization. It's
not all a bad thing. In fact, it can be one way God works for good
the abuse and rejection we may have known as children. It can also,
however, cause us to live life as someone who is driven rather than
led.

How do we find the balance and maintain it? In a profession
that is so competitive, where our very best is more likely to meet

with rejection than acceptance, how do we keep on keeping on? What is the difference between being led by his Spirit rather than driven by our need for recognition and success?

"I surrender all," I publicly proclaimed when I was baptized as an adult. After a brief testimony, I read aloud the words of J. W. Van DeVenter's powerful hymn with that title:

> All to Jesus I surrender,
> All to Him I freely give;
> I will ever love and trust Him,
> In His presence daily live.
>
> All to Jesus I surrender,
> Humbly at His feet I bow,
> Worldly pleasures all forsaken,
> Take me, Jesus, take me now.
>
> All to Jesus I surrender,
> Make me, Savior, wholly Thine;
> Let me feel the Holy Spirit,
> Truly know that Thou art mine.
>
> All to Jesus I surrender,
> Lord, I give myself to Thee;
> Fill me with Thy love and power,
> Let Thy blessing fall on me.

It was a life-changing experience, and one that I need to keep coming back to as I struggle with the business/ministry tension of being in full-time Christian work. It's so easy to take my eyes off the Lord. I begin to worry (I'm so good at it!) about paying the bills and making a mark in the world of Christian publishing. Instead of being led and empowered by God's Spirit, all too frequently I drive myself to make things happen in my own strength. I run ahead of the Lord and lose the joy he wants me to experience each and every day.

"Oh, that we might know the Lord! Let us press on to know him, and he will respond to us as surely as the coming of dawn or the rain of early spring," Hosea said (Hos. 6:3). Twenty-eight centuries later, there's no better counsel I can give myself or you. Knowing the Lord needs to be our focus, our passion, our heart's greatest desire. It's only out of the overflow of our relationship with him that we have anything worthwhile to say or write. And it's only as we learn what it means to surrender all that we discover the joy of being led instead of driven.

J. W. Van DeVenter wrote "I Surrender All" out of his own struggle to say yes to God's call to become an evangelist. "For five years he wavered between this challenge and his ambition to become a recognized artist," Billy Graham wrote about this man who influenced his early preaching (*Crusader Hymns and Hymn Stories* edited by Cliff Barrows, Chicago: Hope Publishing, 1967, p. 117). It seems to me his impact on Billy Graham is reason enough to give serious consideration to the words of this hymn.

"All to him I freely give." The driven writer claims ownership of the words he writes and his career, rather than acknowledging the Lordship of Christ. Instead of being "content whatever the circumstances" (Phil. 4:11, NIV)—published or unpublished, well known or obscure—he covets success. It happens so subtly. Without accountability partners who are not afraid to speak truth into our lives, we may not even realize we are in danger of forsaking our first love (Rev. 2:4).

"Humbly at His feet I bow." The driven writer draws her identity from how many manuscripts she sells, how high her published books rank on the best-seller list, royalty statements, and reviews. No wonder she is up one day and down the next and always striving, always driving to produce manuscripts that will win accolades. Shamelessly, she promotes herself and looks for ways to push herself into the spotlight.

Am I saying that striving to become the best possible writer is wrong? That it's wrong to push ourselves to work when it would be easier to procrastinate? That it's wrong to promote our books and speaking ministries? Of course not, for it is God himself who puts within us the drive to serve him and be the best we can be so Jesus Christ will be glorified. But we need to regularly examine our hearts. Do we desire to point others to Christ or ourselves? And do we realize that without him we are nothing? The apostle Paul asks, "What do you have that God hasn't given you? And if all you have is from God, why act as though you are so great, and as though you have accomplished something on your own?" (1 Cor. 4:7).

"Make me, Savior, wholly Thine." This line reminds me that he is the potter and I am the clay. "Does the pot argue with its maker? Does the clay dispute with him who forms it, saying, 'Stop, you're doing it wrong!'" (Isa. 45:9). If God chooses for me to be a best-selling, A-list author, praise his name. If only a B-list author or wannabe, then praise his name anyway. He is Lord, and he knows the plans he has for me (Jer. 29:11). My part is simply to be faithful.

I know I'm driven when I try to force God's hand and tell him what to do. But when I choose to be led by God, I don't need to look to the left or to the right to see what others are doing. I don't need to try to keep pace with them. Instead, I'm at peace doing what he has commanded *me* to do. And he gives me the assurance that all that happens to me is working for my good if I love him and am fitting into his plans (Rom. 8:28).

"Lord, I give myself to Thee." This line speaks to me of my need to be wholeheartedly committed to the Lord and to *his* plan for my life and writing. To be honest, I'm not always there. I need "to put aside [my] own desires so that [I] will become patient and godly, gladly letting God have his way with [me]" (2 Pet. 1:6). Praise God, he also promises: "The more you go on in this way, the more you will grow strong spiritually and become fruitful and useful to our Lord Jesus Christ" (v. 8). Isn't that what Van DeVenter had in mind in his last line: "Let Thy blessing fall on me"? It may not be what we would have proposed to the Lord. No, it will be far better—but only as we surrender all and choose to be led rather than driven.

—————

RESPONDING TO GOD'S CALL TO WRITE

Sometimes our drivenness comes from fear that we will not measure up to what God expects of us. Like the apostle Paul, we may try to earn our salvation. Read about his experience in Philippians 3:4-14. Then take time to examine your own heart. Ask the Lord to show you whether you are driven or led. Then, if you are ready, sing or read the words of "I Surrender All" as a prayer.

32

Count It All Joy

Consider it pure joy, my brothers,
whenever you face trials of many kinds.
JAMES 1:2, NIV

You've got to be kidding me! Rejoice in my trials? It's one of those seeming contradictions that cause some unbelievers to look at Christians as if we have a few screws loose. Others find themselves strangely drawn to the unexplainable joy we possess despite difficulties.

I've never forgotten reading, as a teenager, that stirring climatic scene in *The Robe* by Lloyd C. Douglas. In my mind's eye, I can see Diana going to stand beside her beloved Marcellus who has been accused by the emperor Caligula of "consorting with a party of revolutionists known as Christians" (Boston: Houghton Mifflin Company, 1942, p. 606).

"I, too, am a Christian," she proclaims. When the emperor insists she is not being tried, courageously she adds: "If it please Your Majesty, may I then provide evidence to warrant a conviction? I have no wish to live another hour in an Empire so far along on the road to ruin that it would consent to be governed by one who has no interest in the welfare of his people. . . . As for me—I have another King—and I desire to go with my husband—into that Kingdom!" (p. 611).

With heads held high and smiles on their faces, Diana and
Marcellus walk to their deaths and to life everlasting.

Is my faith that strong? Do I have that kind of courage?
Hopefully I'll never have to answer those questions. I have no desire
to be a martyr! I do desire, however, with all my heart to be found
faithful.

"Consider it pure joy, my brothers, whenever you face trials of
many kinds, because you know that the testing of your faith develops perseverance," James wrote. "Perseverance must finish its work
so that you may be mature and complete, not lacking anything"
(James 1:2-4, NIV).

To be honest, I'd prefer to skip the trials and be just a little less
mature! I get weary of being on the growing edge, weary of having
my faith tested. And yet if this is what it takes for me to "grow strong
spiritually and become fruitful and useful to our Lord Jesus Christ"
(2 Pet. 1:8), I don't want to wimp out.

Years ago, I remember sitting in my pastor's study and telling
him how discouraged I was because of the rejection slips I had been
receiving. "But if God does not allow your faith to be tested, how
will you be prepared to stand when the stakes are really big?" my
pastor asked me.

It wasn't what I wanted to hear, but I knew he was right. There
really are no shortcuts to becoming strong in the Lord.

But where's the joy in all the trials? Does following Christ and
seeking to write his answer mean that we're always being put to the
test? That life is always intense and serious? That joy and laughter is
something we never experience? Absolutely not!

The psalmist says we are to "shout for joy" (Ps. 33:3, NIV). We
are to "sing for joy to God our strength" (Ps. 81:1, NIV). Even "the
mountains sing together for joy" (Ps. 98:8, NIV). And "the trees of
the field will clap their hands" (Isa. 55:12, NIV). Amen!

Years ago, a wise friend encouraged me to make a blessing jar.
"Write down every blessing you can think of on a separate slip of
paper. Then fold it, and put it in a jar," she said. "When you are feeling
down, take one blessing at a time out of the jar and thank God for it."

What can we put in our blessing jars today? What has he
promised to us? What are some reasons to rejoice even when we
may be getting more rejections than acceptances? Here are a few:

- "I will instruct you (says the Lord) and guide you along the best pathway for your life; I will advise you and watch your progress. Abiding love surrounds those who trust in the Lord. So rejoice in him, all those who are his, and shout for joy, all those who try to obey him" (Ps. 32:8, 10-11).
- "The joy of the Lord is [our] strength" (Neh. 8:10).
- "Those who sow tears shall reap joy" (Ps. 126:5).
- With his enabling, our "words can be a source of wisdom, deep as the ocean, fresh as a flowing stream" (Prov. 18:4, TEV).
- "God's gifts and his call can never be withdrawn; he will never go back on his promises" (Rom. 11:29).
- He has given us "the wonderful privilege of telling everyone about this plan of his" (Eph. 3:7).
- "Out of his glorious, unlimited resources he will give [us] the mighty inner strengthening of his Holy Spirit" (Eph. 3:16).

Wow! Those are indeed reasons to rejoice. And in times of testing, we can also rejoice for he promises that "he will not allow [us] to be tested beyond [our] power to remain firm; at the time [we] are put to the test, he will give [us] the strength to endure" (1 Cor. 10:13, TEV).

The first words I ever felt God speak to my spirit were, "I've never promised it would be easy to follow me, but I have promised always to be with you." Of course there are times when I doubt, times when I feel alone and overwhelmed. But again and again God has reminded me, "Child, I am with you."

Paul wrote, "We can rejoice, too, when we run into problems and trials for we know that they are good for us—they help us learn to be patient. And patience develops strength of character in us and helps us trust God more each time we use it until finally our hope and faith are strong and steady" (Rom. 5:3-4).

I'm still a long way from where God wants me to be. Patience is not one of my strengths, and grumbling comes more naturally than rejoicing. Obviously, God has more work to do in me. But I can count it all joy because nothing can be "compared to the surpassing greatness of knowing Christ Jesus my Lord" (Phil. 3:8, NIV).

RESPONDING TO GOD'S CALL TO WRITE

Make your own "blessing jar" and dig into it frequently to help you not to overlook the blessings in the midst of the trials and testings that come with being a Christian and serving the Lord through the ministry of writing.

REJOICE, THE LORD IS KING
by Charles Wesley

Rejoice the Lord is King! Your Lord and King adore!
Rejoice, give thanks, and sing, And triumph evermore:
Lift up your heart, lift up your voice!
Rejoice, again I say, rejoice!

The Lord, our Savior, reigns, The God of truth and love;
When He had purged our stains, He took His seat above:
Lift up your heart, lift up your voice!
Rejoice, again I say, rejoice!

His kingdom cannot fail, He rules o'er earth and heav'n;
The keys of death and hell Are to our Jesus giv'n:
Lift up your heart, lift up your voice!
Rejoice, again I say, rejoice!

Rejoice in glorious hope! Our Lord the judge shall come
And take His servants up To their eternal home:
Lift up your heart, lift up your voice!
Rejoice, again I say, rejoice!

(Charles Wesley was a prolific writer of hymns. Over 4,500 of his hymns were published with another 3,000 in manuscript form. The chorus of this one is based on Philippians 4:4.)

33

Proclaiming Truth to a Dying World

≥⊙

Let us encourage one another—
and all the more as you see
the Day approaching.
HEBREWS 10:25, NIV

I had just given one of my Christian writers' seminars in our nation's capital. Many of the people who attended made commitments to write God's answer. Fervently, I prayed for them and myself that we would be faithful to God's call.

That evening, my hostess took me on a tour of the city. I had been to D.C. several times during the day but never at night. In the moonlight, the buildings were even more magnificent. But I was not an awestruck tourist taking in the sights. Rather, I began to grieve. It was as if God were showing me the heartbeat of my nation, and the heartbeat was weak.

As we left the city an hour later, we drove past the Lincoln Memorial. "Child, not one stone will be left standing on another," I felt the Lord speak to my heart. Never have I been so aware of his presence, so sure of his voice. I wept for the city and my nation.

"Are you sure it was the Lord?" people have asked me. "I wish I thought it wasn't him," I've replied. Only time will tell. What I do know is that Jesus is coming—perhaps soon, perhaps in my lifetime and yours. And I know there is an eternal truth in what he said before his crucifixion. "As long as it is day, we must do the work of him who sent me. Night is coming, when no one can work" (John 9:4, NIV).

As I write this chapter, millennium fever has even non-Christians believing that history is moving to a climax. So many pieces of the end-times puzzle are falling into place. World peace hangs by a slender thread, especially in the Holy Land where ailing Middle East leaders who have kept a tenuous peace may soon be forced to step down. Only God knows the changes new leadership will bring.

Technology now exists for the mark of the beast. The anticipated computer crisis surrounding the year 2000 could certainly set the stage for the Antichrist to step forward as the apparent savior. Or maybe you're reading this after 2000 (I hope you are), but now another seemingly unsolvable crisis looms on the horizon.

I am not about to set a date for the Lord's return or pretend to be an eschatologist. Most of Revelation and Daniel remain a mystery to me. I've read a couple of end-times novels and really don't care to read more. The scenario of what may be right around the corner could make for sleepless nights, especially since I don't know whether the Rapture will be pretribulation, midtribulation, or post tribulation. My gut-level feeling is that God isn't going to zap us out of the dark days that are coming when the light of Christ's love will be most desperately needed. But I may be wrong. So may the pre-trib crowd. Again, only God knows.

Even Jesus said, "No one knows the date and hour when the end will be—not even the angels. No, nor even God's Son. Only the Father knows" (Matt. 24:36).

So what *do* we know in these days of uncertainty? Where *do* we find security as the financial crisis in other nations creates havoc on the New York Stock Exchange and threatens whatever nest egg we may have been able to accumulate? How do we let our lights shine in the encroaching darkness?

"Be prepared, for you don't know what day your Lord is coming" (Matt. 24:42). Just as no one expected (at least I certainly didn't) that the USSR would collapse or the Berlin Wall crumble, the Lord's coming will be just as unexpected. "The world will be at ease—banquets and parties and weddings—just as it was in

Noah's time before the sudden coming of the flood; people wouldn't believe what was going to happen until the flood actually arrived and took them all away. So shall my coming be," Jesus said (Matt. 24:37-39). We need to live in a state of expectancy rather than allow ourselves to be lulled into a business-as-usual, laid-back approach to the work of ministry.

"Stay true to the Lord," the apostle Paul wrote from a Roman prison (Phil. 4:1). If we are to proclaim truth to our dying world, it is critically important that we understand what truth is. More than ever before, we need to be grounded in his Word, so if it were to be taken from us, it would, indeed, be buried deep in our hearts. Not only do we need to know the truth, we have to be committed to the truth, regardless of the price tag. Now is *not* the time to compromise, not the time to bow the knee to any other god than the Lord Jesus Christ. No matter how harmless it may seem to "bend just a little" so as not to offend, not to be seen as a fanatic, we must never forget that Jesus said, "I am the Way—yes, and the Truth and the Life. No one can get to the Father except by means of me" (John 14:6).

"Let not your heart be troubled," Jesus said. "You are trusting God, now trust in me" (John 14:1). Even though the world as we have known it may seem to be spinning out of control, we need to remember that none of what is happening is taking God by surprise. He is still in control! He is "the Alpha and the Omega, the Beginning and the End" (Rev. 21:6, NIV). And despite the turmoil around us, he promises the gift of peace of mind and heart (John 14:27). We do not need to fear nor be consumed by worry. He has promised not to abandon us or leave us as "orphans in the storm" (John 14:18).

Yes, the future seems frightening. The unknown strikes fear in many people. But as Christians, we do not need to get caught up in dire doomsday predictions. We know how it all ends! "Hallelujah! Salvation and glory and power belong to our God" (Rev. 19:1, NIV). We can and must "hold unswervingly to the hope we profess, for he who promised is faithful" (Heb. 10:23, NIV). In his strength and through his power, we can lay aside all our self-doubts and feelings of inadequacy and boldly write his answer.

RESPONDING TO GOD'S CALL TO WRITE

Read the letters to the seven churches in Revelation 2 and 3, asking the Lord to speak to you and strengthen you for the work he is calling you to do. Record what he says to you in the space below.

RE-CREATION

And God will say,
"Let there be light.
Let the darkness of evil
no longer reign.
Let there no longer be
thorns and thistles,
sin, death, and decay.
Let there be a new heaven and earth.
Let the home of God
be among his people.
Let all tears be wiped away.
Let the thirsty drink
from the spring
of the Water of Life.
Let all creation rejoice
in the salvation of the Lord."

(Based on Genesis 2:3; Romans 8:20-21; Revelation 21:1-6.)

Appendix 1

≈≈≈

Called to Write His Answer

And the Lord said to me,
"Write my answer on a billboard, large and clear,
so that anyone can read it at a glance
and rush to tell the others."
HABAKKUK 2:2

"And the Lord said to me"

Press on to know the Lord (Hos. 6:3).

Make time to allow the Lord to speak to you through his Word (Ps. 1:2; 2 Tim. 3:16-17; James 1:25).

Seek the Lord's counsel and wisdom (Pss. 16:7; 32:8; Prov. 2:3-10; Isa. 50:4; James 1:5-8).

Wait for God's answer (Hab. 2:1).

Let his words sink into your heart first (Ezek. 3:10-11); then write what you have experienced (1 John 1:3).

"Write my answer"

Diligently study the Word (2 Tim. 2:15).

Remember God's promise that his Word does not return void (Isa. 55:10-11).

Put on God's armor (Eph. 6:10-18).

Make the most of your opportunities (Eph. 5:15-17; Phil. 2:14-16; Col. 4:5-6; 2 Tim. 4:2), knowing that the doors may not always be open (Amos 8:11-12).

Make it "large and clear"

Write to be understood and to make the Gospel clear (1 Cor. 2:1-5).

Let the Holy Spirit do the convicting; don't preach (1 Cor. 2:4; Heb. 4:12).

Know your audience (1 Cor. 2:6).

Work hard (Col. 3:23-25) and enthusiastically (Rom. 12:11) so you do not need to be ashamed of your work (2 Tim. 2:15) or to compare it with others (Gal. 6:4).

Write "so that anyone can read it"

Share the Good News around the world (Ps. 96:1-3; Matt. 28:19-20).

Following Christ's example, minister to the poor, brokenhearted, captives, blind, downtrodden (Luke 4:18-19).

Use illustrations readers can relate to (Mark 4:33-34).

"At a glance"

Have a clear focus; know what you believe and clearly communicate it (2 Tim. 2:8; Titus 3:3-8).

Capture the reader's attention and create reader identification (Mark 4:2).

"And rush to tell the others"

Write so readers will want to pass on your words. Be loving and winsome (1 Thess. 2:7-8; James 3:17).

Provide a take-away so readers will not ask, "So what?" (James 1:22).

Avoid clichés, pat answers, and theological jargon (1 Cor. 1:17).

"Slowly, steadily, surely"

Seek God's plan for your writing (Jer. 29:11-13).

Set specific and measurable goals (Prov. 16:9).

Get to work (1 Chron. 28:20).

Abide in Christ (John 15:4-8).

Keep expecting God to help you; walk (and write) in his strength (Ps. 71:14, 16).

Give yourself and your writing time to develop (Rom. 5:2; Phil. 1:6; Col. 2:7; 2 Pet. 1:2-9).

Have faith (Matt. 21:21-22; John 14:12-14; Heb. 11:1).

Finish what you start (2 Cor. 8:10-11).

Do *not* give in to discouragement and despair (Gal. 6:9).

Appendix 2

Laying a Biblical Foundation for Your Writing Ministry

I will press on to know the Lord (Hos. 6:3), abide in him (John 15:1-8), and keep on growing in him (Col. 2:6-7; 2 Pet. 1:2-9).

I will keep my eyes on Jesus, my leader and instructor (Heb. 12:2).

I will diligently study God's Word in order to become an effective communicator of his truth (2 Tim. 2:15; 3:16-17).

I will daily seek the infilling of the Holy Spirit (Acts 1:8; Eph. 5:18).

I will spend time in prayer, especially in learning to be still and to listen to what God may want to say to me and through me (Pss. 5:3; 46:10; Hab. 2:1; 1 Cor. 2:15-16).

I will make a commitment to private and corporate worship (Ps. 99:5; Heb. 10:25).

I will seek God's direction for my life and my writing (Ps. 32:8; Jer. 29:11-13; Gal. 5:16; James 1:5-8).

I will be sensitive to needs around me and say "yes" to God's call to write his answer (Hab. 2:2).

I will wait on God's empowering (Ps. 40:1-3; Isa. 40:29-31; Col. 1:29).

I will use the gift God has given me and work hard (1 Tim. 4:14-16; 2 Tim. 2:15; 1 Pet. 4:10-11).

I will set specific, measurable goals (Prov. 16:9).

I will reach out to other Christian writers, both to give and receive support and encouragement (Gal. 6:2; 1 Thess. 5:11).

I will humble myself before the Lord and ask forgiveness for my sins that I might be a cleansed vessel through which his power can flow (Prov. 28:13; James 4:7-10; 1 Pet. 5:6; 1 John 1:8-10).

I will put on God's armor (Eph. 6:10-18) and stand firm when the Evil One attacks (1 Pet. 5:8-9).

I will ask for wisdom in setting daily priorities and keeping my life in balance (Prov. 2:3-10).

I will battle procrastination (Eccl. 5:7), get to work (1 Chron. 28:20), and finish what I start (2 Cor. 8:10-11).

I will stay awake and be prepared for Christ's return (Matt. 25:13) and make the most of every opportunity (Col. 4:5).

I will see the rough times in my life as opportunities to grow (Rom. 5:3-5; James 1:2-4) and to pass on to others God's help and comfort (2 Cor. 1:3-7).

I will seek first God's kingdom and his righteousness (Matt. 6:33; Luke 12:31) and trust him to supply all my needs (Phil. 4:19).

I will not get discouraged and give up (Gal. 6:9) but instead will persist and trust God's perfect timing (Pss. 27:14; 37:7; 42:11; Eccl. 3:1; Hab. 2:3; Heb. 11:1).

I will affirm that now I have "every grace and blessing; every spiritual gift and power for doing his will" (1 Cor. 1:7) and expect God to do great things through his power at work within me (Eph. 3:20).

Appendix 3

~~

Writing Your Testimony

1. DO write to encourage others, to give them something to take away and apply to their own lives (2 Cor. 1:3-7; 1 Thess. 5:11).

2. DO make your message clear and direct, your focus sharp. You should be able to state in *one* sentence what you hope to communicate to your readers (Col. 1:20, 28).

3. DO be in touch with people and their needs, not preoccupied with yourself (Phil. 2:4). Make your writing relevant and timely.

4. DO point your readers to Christ, not to yourself (1 Cor. 2:2-5).

5. DO write with conviction and enthusiasm (Rom. 1:16).

6. DO let your words be gracious as well as sensible (Col. 4:6).

7. DO back up your experience with Scripture (or scriptural principles). DON'T prooftext, quote inaccurately, or quote excessively (2 Tim. 2:15).

8. DON'T preach! Let the Holy Spirit do the convicting (John 16:8).

9. DO write with love and sensitivity. Avoid pat and simplistic answers, but DON'T water down the power of the Gospel. Gently lead your readers to the Answer (1 Thess. 1:7-8).

10. DO be honest, open, and vulnerable. Take off your mask. Be real. Let the reader see your struggles (Rom. 7:15-25).

11. DON'T write it too soon. Wait for objectivity and perspective (Gal. 1:15-18). Live it first, but DON'T let the enemy silence your witness because you're not perfect (Phil. 3:12).

12. DON'T try to cover too long a time frame. Avoid unnecessary tangents or characters. Share the right amount of your life before Christ—not too much, not too little (1 Tim. 1:15-16).

13. DO be led by the Holy Spirit and trust him to give you the right words (1 Cor. 1:7) and to strengthen you in your weakness (2 Cor. 12:9-10).

14. DON'T be surprised or defeated by ridicule and persecution (1 Pet. 5:8-11).

15. DON'T put family or friends in an embarrassing position by writing about them without their permission. Use a pseudonym when appropriate and requested (Eph. 5:21).

16. DO keep rewriting until it's your very best work (2 Tim. 2:15).

17. DON'T get discouraged! Keep submitting your manuscript, so it will "reap a harvest of blessing" (Gal. 6:9).

Appendix 4

From Idea to Published Manuscript

1. Train yourself to find ideas in the Scriptures, life experiences, history, nature, the media, etc.

2. Capture your idea immediately by writing it down. Keep a journal.

3. File your ideas where they can be found. Develop a corresponding resource file.

4. Ask yourself which ideas you feel most compelled to develop.

5. Pray about your ideas. Ask the Lord to help you weed out the "fluff" and to show you which should take priority. Work them into your "Goal Planning Chart" (page 26).

6. Research the market. (See "Recommended Resources," page 167.)

7. Before you begin writing, picture your readers and pray for them.

8. Determine the best format for your idea—story, article, devotional, poem, or perhaps even a book. Be realistic. Learn the best opportunities by networking with other writers.

9. Do the necessary research. Quote accurately and get permission when needed.

10. Outline or develop a plan for your manuscript.

11. Write and rewrite as many times as necessary until you are certain this manuscript is your very best work. If at all possible, attend a writers' group and have your manuscript critiqued. See Sally Stuart's *Christian Writers' Market Guide* for a list of groups.

12. Ask yourself: Do I have a clear theme or story line? Is my idea tightly focused and well organized? Is there reader identification and a strong take-away? Have I been open, honest, vulnerable? Did I show or tell? Teach or preach?

13. Resist the temptation to mail your manuscript too soon. Let it cool for at least a week. Live it!

14. Put your best foot forward. Show you have carefully studied the market by submitting a manuscript that will meet editorial needs. Be sure to use the proper manuscript format and enclose a SASE (self-addressed, stamped envelope).

15. Do the needed record keeping to keep track of submissions.

16. As you mail your manuscript, release it to the Lord. Then get to work on your next writing project. Be sure to get a receipt from the post office, and note the amount in your log of writing expenses/earnings.

17. If your manuscript is returned, resubmit it immediately to the next market on your list.

18. After publication, pray for the editor and his ministry and for the people who will read your printed piece. Learn all you can from the changes the editor made. Send a brief thank-you letter and another manuscript or query. Be a good steward by marketing reprints if you have not sold all rights.

19. Do not give in to the deadly Ds—disappointment, discouragement, doubt, and despair. Look to Jesus. Remember he never promised it would be easy to follow him. Claim the promise of Galatians 6:9 and persevere.

20. Keep developing your skills. Keep growing. Attend writing seminars and conferences. (See the list in the *Christian Writers' Market Guide.*) Consider enrolling in a correspondence course. (See "Recommended Resources," page 167.)

Appendix 5

A Writer's Statement of Faith

"I have strength for all things in Christ Who empowers me—I am ready for anything and equal to anything through Him Who infuses inner strength into me, [that is, I am self-sufficient in Christ's sufficiency]" (Phil. 4:13, AMP).

I will write with "all the strength and energy that God supplies, so that God will be glorified through Jesus Christ" (1 Pet. 4:11).

"[Not in my own strength] for it is God Who is all the while effectually at work in {me}—energizing and creating in {me} the power and desire—both to will and to work for His good pleasure and satisfaction and delight" (Phil. 2:13, AMP).

My "strength must come from the Lord's mighty power within [me]" (Eph. 6:10).

"In Him in every respect {I am} enriched, in full power and readiness of speech (to speak {and write} of {my} faith), and complete knowledge and illumination (to give {me} full insight into its meaning)" (1 Cor. 1:5, AMP).

"Now [I] have every grace and blessing; every spiritual gift and power for doing his will are [mine] during this time of waiting for the return of our Lord Jesus Christ" (1 Cor. 1:7).

I "actually do have within [me] a portion of the very thoughts and mind of Christ" (1 Cor. 2:16).

I can be a mirror "that brightly reflect[s] the glory of the Lord" (2 Cor. 3:18).

I will "commit everything [I] do to the Lord." I will "trust him to help [me] do it and he will" (Ps. 37:5).

I will "lean on, trust and be confident in the Lord with all {my} heart and mind, and {choose not to} rely on {my} own insight or understanding" (Prov. 3:5, AMP).

I will "commit [my] work to the Lord, then it will succeed" (Prov. 16:3).

Writing is my work, "and I can do it only because Christ's mighty energy is at work within me" (Col. 1:29).

I will "be strong and courageous and get to work." I will not "be frightened by the size of the task, for the Lord my God is with [me]; he will not forsake [me]. He will see to it that everything is finished correctly" (1 Chron. 28:20).

I need to "keep on patiently doing God's will if [I] want him to do for [me] all he has promised" (Heb. 10:36).

"I am convinced and sure of this very thing, that He Who began a good work in {me} will continue until the day of Jesus Christ— right up to the time of His return—developing [that good work] and perfecting and bringing it to full completion in {me}" (Phil. 1:6, AMP).

"His mighty power at work within [me] is able to do far more than [I] would ever dare to ask or even dream of—infinitely beyond [my] highest prayers, desires, thoughts, or hopes" (Eph. 3:20).

Appendix 6

Helps for Forming Critique Groups

God is calling an army of writers, and he can use you to help equip them. "How?" you wonder, especially if you a beginning writer yourself. The Lord promises that when two or three gather in his name he will be with them (Matt. 18:20). I know he will honor his promise as you choose to make him the center of your group. But how do you go about forming a group?

STARTING A GROUP

The Greater Philadelphia Christian Writers' Fellowship began in 1983 through an article that was printed in several community newspapers and announcements that were sent to churches. To be honest, we received more support from the newspapers. Unless you have a personal contact in a church (or follow up the announcement of the formation of your group with a visit or phone call), it's likely it will be round-filed because of the tremendous volume of mail a church receives.

Ask your church to pray for you and help publicize the group in the Sunday morning bulletin and/or church newsletter. You may also want to do mini posters for your church and neighboring churches. But again you'll probably need to personally deliver them (or have a friend who is a member deliver them).

Keep newspaper announcements concise. Tell when and where you're meeting. (Your home or a church are the best locations.) State your purpose and what will be expected of those who come. For example, "Bring a manuscript to read and the desire to improve your writing." Give your name and phone number for more information.

For more help and encouragement to start a group or to learn about my Christian Writers' Seminar that God has used to launch groups, please feel free to e-mail me (mbagnull@aol.com) or call me (610-626-6833).

Appendix 7

The Critique Process

Realizing that the critiquing process can be very threatening, here are some guidelines.

Guidelines for Critiquers

1. Ask God for discernment and sensitivity.

2. Find something positive to say about the manuscript *before* making suggestions for change.

3. Respect one another's beliefs. Do *not* debate theology.

4. Use a checkoff list to consider various aspects of the manuscripts. You won't help the writer by a casual critique and the comment that "it's wonderful."

5. As much as possible, give equal time to all who have manuscripts to read.

6. Try to suggest possible markets.

7. Strive always to be honest encouragers.

GUIDELINES FOR THE PERSON BEING CRITIQUED

1. Have someone else read your manuscript. Hearing your manuscript read aloud is a wonderful way of picking up on problem areas.

2. If possible, bring copies of your manuscript. It is often much easier for others to spot problem areas when they can see as well as hear it being read.

3. Be open to new thoughts and ideas.

4. Listen. Do *not* debate or argue or defend your work.

5. Pray about the suggestions you've received.

6. Be accountable to work with your manuscript (or with another writing project if you determine the manuscript you have read is not worth pursuing) in order to be a good steward of the group's time.

7. "Commit your work to the Lord, then it will succeed" (Prov. 16:3).

Appendix 8

Goals for Christian Writers' Groups

The following goals have guided the Greater Philadelphia Christian Writers' Fellowship since our formation in 1983. You are welcome to use or adapt them. With God's help we are endeavoring to:

1. Press on to know the Lord, abide in him, and keep on growing in him (Hos. 6:3; John 15:1- 8; Col. 2:7).

2. Reach out to one another in fellowship, support, understanding, and encouragement (Phil. 2:4; 1 Thess. 5:11; Gal. 6:2).

3. Pray for one another—for our personal needs, our writing, and especially God's guidance and enabling (Eph. 6:18-19; Col. 4:2; 1 Tim. 2:1).

4. Increase our knowledge of God's Word in order to become effective communicators of his truth (Ezek. 3:10-11; 2 Tim. 2:15; 3:16-17).

5. Strengthen our writing and marketing skills (1 Tim. 4:14-15).

6. Develop strong working relationships with editors and undergird them with prayer (Rom. 12:4-5; Eph. 4:12-13).

7. Keep abreast of current issues. Look for opportunities to write his answer (Hab. 2:2; Col. 4:5- 6).

8. Battle procrastination and "get to work" (1 Chron. 28:20).

9. Learn to persevere and overcome discouragement (1 Cor. 15:58; Hab. 2:3; Gal. 6:9).

10. Expect God to do mighty things in and through us (Eph. 3:20).

Appendix 9

~~◈~~

Recommended Resources

Magazines and Newsletters

Advanced Christian Writer. P.O. Box 110390, Nashville, TN 37222. Bi-monthly newsletter of American Christian Writers. Web site: www.ecpa.org/acw.

The Christian Communicator. P.O. Box 110390, Nashville, TN 37222. Monthly magazine of American Christian Writers. Web site: www.ecpa.org/acw.

Cross & Quill. Route 3, Box 1635, Jefferson Davis Road, Clinton, SC 29325-9542. Bi-monthly publication of Christian Writers Fellowship International. Web site: http://members.aol.com/cwfi/writers.htm.

WIN Informer. P.O. Box 11337, Bainbridge Island, WA 98110. Bi-monthly magazine of Writers Information Network, The Professional Association for Christian Writers. Web sites: www.bluejaypub.com/win or www.ecpa.org/win.

Books

1,818 Ways to Write Better & Get Published by Scott Edelstein. Cincinnati: Writer's Digest Books, 1991.

Awakening the Giant: Mobilizing and Equipping Christians to Reclaim Our Nation in This Generation by Jim Russell. Grand Rapids: Zondervan Publishing House, 1996.

Christian Cyberspace Companion by Jason D. Baker. Grand Rapids: Baker Book House, 1997.

The Christian Writer's Book: A Practical Guide to Writing by Don M. Aycock and Leonard G. Goss. New Brunswick, NJ: Bridge-Logos Publishers, 1996.

A Christian Writer's Manual of Style by Bob Hudson and Shelley Townsend. Grand Rapids: Zondervan Publishing House, 1988.

Christian Writers' Market Guide by Sally Stuart. Wheaton, IL: Harold Shaw Publishers, annually.

The Complete Guide to Christian Writing and Speaking edited by Susan Titus Osborn. Orange, CA: Promise Publishing, 1994. Available from the editor, 3133 Puente Street, Fullerton, CA 92835-1952.

The Complete Guide to Writing & Selling the Christian Novel by Penelope J. Stokes. Cincinnati: Writer's Digest Books, 1998.

A Complete Guide to Writing for Publication edited by Susan Titus Osborn. Phoenix: ACW Press, 1999.

Freedom from Tyranny of the Urgent by Charles E. Hummel. Downers Grove, IL: InterVarsity Press, 1997.

Introduction to Christian Writing (Revised) by Ethel Herr. Phoenix: ACW Press, 1999.

On Writing Well by William Zinsser. New York: HarperReference, 1998.

The Persuasive Person: Communicating More Effectively in Person and in Print by JamesWatkins. Indianapolis: Wesley Press, 1987.

Publish Your Own Novel by Connie Shelton. Angel Fire, NM: Columbine Books, 1996.

Roaring Lambs: A Gentle Plan to Radically Change Your World by Bob Briner. Grand Rapids: Zondervan Publishing House, 1993.

The Scott, Foresman Handbook for Writers by Maxine Hairston et al. Reading, MA: Addison-Wesley Publishing Company, 1998.

Time Management for the Creative Person by Lee Silber. New York: Three Rivers Press, 1998.

Top 50 Magazine Publishers' Marketing Packet by Sally E. Stuart. Compiled yearly. Available from the author, 1647 SW Pheasant Drive, Aloha, OR 97006.

Writing Articles From the Heart—How to Write and Sell Your Life Experiences by Marjorie Holmes. Cincinnati: Writer's Digest Books, 1993.

Writing Together: How to Transform Your Writing in a Writing Group by Dawn Denham Haines, Susan Newcomer, and Jacqueline Raphael. New York: Perigee Books, 1997.

You Can Do It: A Guide to Christian Self-Publishing by Athena Dean. Mukilteo, WA: WinePress Publishing, 1998.

CORRESPONDENCE COURSES

American School of Writing. American Christian Writers, P.O. Box 110390, Nashville, TN 37222.

At-Home Writing Workshops. Marlene Bagnull, instructor. 316 Blanchard Road, Drexel Hill, PA 19026. Web site: http://nancepub.com/cwf/.

The Christian Communicator Hands-on Course (e-mail or cassette). Susan Titus Osborn, instructor. 3133 Puente Street, Fullerton, CA 92835-1952. E-mail: Susanosb@aol.com. Web site: www.christiancommunicator.com.

Christian Writers Guild. Norman Rohrer, director. 65287 Fern Street, Hume, CA 93628-9611.

Christian Writers Institute. P.O. Box 110390, Nashville, TN 37222.

Poetry Writing Sessions. Mary Harwell Sayler, instructor. P.O. Box 730, DeLand, FL 32721.

ALSO BY THE AUTHOR

ABC's of Marketing. How-tos of market research and analysis, best opportunities, five market analysis charts, and more.

Tapes on a variety of writing related topics.

For more information:
Marlene Bagnull, 316 Blanchard Road, Drexel Hill, PA 19026. E-mail: mbagnull@aol.com. Web site: http://nancepub.com/cwf/.

*"Slowly, steadily, surely,
the time approaches when the vision
will be fulfilled.
If it seems slow, do not despair,
for these things will surely
come to pass.
Just be patient!
They will not be overdue a single day!"*

Habakkuk 2:3

Order Form

Postal orders:
ACW Press, 5501 N. 7th Ave., Suite 502, Phoenix, AZ 85013

Telephone orders: (800) 931-BOOK (2665)
Visa and Mastercard accepted

Please send Write His Answer to:

Name:_____

Address:_____

City:_____ State:_____

Zip:_____

Telephone: (_____) _____

Book Price: $14.00 in U.S. dollars.

Sales Tax: Please add 6.85% for books shipped to an Arizona
address.

Shipping: $4.00 for the first book and $1.00 for each additional
book to cover shipping and handling within US,
Canada, and Mexico. International orders add $6.00
for the first book and $2.00 for each additional book.

Quantity Discounts Available - Please call for information
(602) 336-8910